MORE THAN
CONQUERORS

"Queen Mary"   N.Y. Harbor

MORE THAN CONQUERORS

a memoir of lost arguments

MEGAN HUSTAD

farrar, straus and giroux   new york

Farrar, Straus and Giroux
18 West 18th Street, New York 10011

Copyright © 2014 by Megan Hustad
Printed in the United States of America
First edition, 2014

Library of Congress Cataloging-in-Publication Data
Hustad, Megan.
    More than conquerors : a memoir of lost arguments / Megan Hustad. —
First edition.
        pages   cm
    ISBN 978-0-374-29883-8 (hardback) — ISBN 978-0-374-71162-7 (ebook)
    1. Hustad, Megan.   2. Hustad, Megan—Family.   3. Evangelicalism—
Social aspects—United States.   4. Evangelicalism—United States—
Psychological aspects.   5. Children of missionaries—United States—
Biography.   6. Religion and social status—United States—Case studies.
7. Social conflict—United States—Case studies.   8. Families—
Religious life—United States—Case studies.   I. Title.

BR1643.H87 A3 2014
269'.2092—dc23
[B]
                                                                                          2013038713

Designed by Jonathan D. Lippincott

Farrar, Straus and Giroux books may be purchased for educational, business,
or promotional use. For information on bulk purchases, please contact the
Macmillan Corporate and Premium Sales Department at 1-800-221-7945,
extension 5442, or write to specialmarkets@macmillan.com.

www.fsgbooks.com
www.twitter.com/fsgbooks • www.facebook.com/fsgbooks

1   3   5   7   9   10   8   6   4   2

Some names have been changed.

MORE THAN CONQUERORS

To my parents, Stan and Karen,

and my parents' parents: Vivian and Wesley Hustad,
Orville and Marian Johnson

The great, terrible, important powers of the world, like social caste and religious domination, always rest on secrets. A man is born on the wrong side of the street and can therefore never enter into certain drawing rooms . . . When you try to find out what the difference is, and why he is accursed, you find that the reason is a secret. It is a secret that a certain kind of straw hat is damnable. Little boys know these things about other little boys. The world is written over with mysterious tramp-languages and symbols of Masonic hieroglyphics.   —John Jay Chapman

The guide said the Americans were very daring people; above all, they liked to risk their lives, they did it frequently, as a matter of course.   —Vilhelm Moberg, *Unto a Good Land*

Besides exterminating the devil, your other dream is to be loved for who you are.
              —George Bernanos, *Diary of a Country Priest*

CONTENTS

PRELUDE

My great-uncle Donald Hustad, who would go on to become the official crusade organist for the evangelist Billy Graham, grew up with my grandfather Wes in a small town called Boone, Iowa, at a home for indigents. They weren't orphans but their father was dead, and the Boone Biblical College and Associated Institutions took their mother, Clara, and these pale, fat-kneed boys in and gave them work and a place to sleep. For pocket money Don helped a man known as Uncle Pete hunt rabbits. Uncle Pete was no one's uncle as far as anyone in Boone could tell, but there they were. Uncle Pete's preferred method for catching rabbits was to send a ferret scrambling down one end of the rabbit warren while Don stood ready at the other opening, waiting for the terrified rabbits to come hurtling out. Then, fast, they snatched them up and wrung their necks and it was all over pretty quickly, bloodlessly. Knocking on doors in the late afternoon, sun cascading over nearby cornfields to stop at low-hanging eaves, Pete and Don managed to sell most of their take.

Sometimes Don took an unsold rabbit home to his mother. But Clara wasn't comfortable accepting gifts from men, especially not Uncle Pete, and as often as not she'd push Don back out the screen door to spread his charity elsewhere. Once she sent him marching, sniffling and sad for reasons he couldn't quite discern, dead rabbit tucked into the crook of his elbow, over to a missionary family staying down the road. This family had just returned from Africa, and after resting up in Iowa would be going back there, because more people needed to hear the good news.

Don knocks, irritation over forced goodness drying his throat.

"We don't eat rabbit," the missionary mom tells him. This was so surprising to Don he remembered it eighty years later.

"I had thought," he said, "that missionaries ate anything."

✦

When we were bored, we rolled over to the side of the road and parked the car in front of an abandoned *kunuku* and ambled over, through whatever remained of the gate, careful not to scratch our legs on barbed wire and cactus bits. These old farmhouses stood vacant and when former inhabitants left, they moved swiftly, leaving most household items behind. A Nescafé mug, dried coffee caked at the bottom; rusty teaspoons; dinged aluminum pots with flame-scorched bottoms; one left sandal; an empty Alberto VO5 shampoo bottle, teeth marks suggesting its transformation into dog toy; gauzy curtains of white lace bleached and brittle from persistent sun, lifted occasionally by the breeze and the only things that moved in these *kunukus*, until we showed up. In the bedrooms, stained mattresses. Outside on the cactus fence, a red rag draped over a goat skull. Those were Keep Out signs for evil spirits, the missionaries who had lived on the island longer told us. It was, my father explained, like how the babies on Bonaire wore stocking caps, and you'd see that and think, *weird*, it's not cold here on this Caribbean island, so why give babies woolly hats?

The answer was: because of the soft spot. People here believed that evil spirits could enter a baby's brain through the soft spot, and after that happened, who knew what other trouble. Once the fontanel grew over, however, the hat could be safely removed.

The natives of Bonaire were superstitious, other missionaries chimed in, and my sister, Amy, had to explain to me what "superstition" meant because I was six years younger and the vocabulary used in family conversations was rarely dumbed down to my level. *It means holding ideas that are not true*, she said. *To think certain things would happen if other things happened first.*

Does that make sense? she asked.

Sure. It was like how you took a running leap into bed at night so the bogeymen beneath couldn't grab your ankles and pull you under.

Kunukus were silent save for the breeze and creak of rusted hinges. We came to scan the dirt and tables and cupboards for treasures. Seashells, marbles, old soda bottles. Sometimes we glued bits of old sea glass onto driftwood and called it crafts and our better efforts we hung on the wall because as our mother said, there wasn't a lot to *do* on Bonaire. Sometimes everything left behind at the *kunuku* was plastic and that was always disappointing.

We glanced back at the Toyota to make sure no one was trying to get into the backseat. Of course if you never wanted to lose a thing, you'd keep it with you, you'd pack it in your carry-on, you'd keep it on your person, because anything left in a car or placed in a suitcase was something that by definition you were okay with losing, if you had to. Like if someone wanted it more.

After a half hour I slumped down at the edge of the porch, wary of nails and splinters, and wiped sweat from my calves and behind my knees and waited for my mother and Amy to finish their search. I always finished first because, I was beginning to suspect, I didn't know how to look. Amy always found better things, and so for a while I thought I should search longer, harder, but still she found better stuff, so I stopped trying.

But why did the people who lived here abandon their *kunuku* in such a hurry? They didn't even push their chairs in.

At some point I pieced together, through snatches of conversation not meant for me, that the reason was death. The owners had convinced themselves that if they stayed a minute longer, they would die. So they up and bolted. They ran for more time. They ran toward a second third fourth chance. As Christians, we knew that they were not alone in their attempt to escape possible futures. They had an audience. Our God watched them from above and he worried, worried they would trip and fall or *smack!* run right into a tree branch and hurt their heads. That is what the God of my childhood did best. He worried. He worried because oh oh dear what messes we made.

✦

Occasionally I meet someone who was raised in a secular home and I am not envious. Far more often I am. I want to crawl into their skin and take on their swagger, their stride. People who weren't raised with the specter of an all-seeing God looking over their shoulder, meaningfully clearing his throat when you're about to make a mistake, are more confident. They must get a lot more done, I imagine, with all the emotional and intellectual energy they save not having to translate from Christianese. Our rhetoric is full of *perhaps*es and *maybe*s, our mind toggles between what we think and ought to be thinking. Second-guessing like daily bread. I imagine the godless live closer to their desires. The reason my great-uncle Don was surprised to hear the missionary woman refuse rabbit was because in his mind—in all our minds—those so devoted to furthering the kingdom of God shouldn't care too much about what they cared about. Personal preferences were luxuries, like guest soaps in guest bathrooms.

My family's brand of Christianity involved many chores.

As overseas missionaries, you make a lot of trips to the airport. You're routinely picking people up from the airport and dropping them off at the airport. This is one reason why we like speaking of the afterlife; we fear we'll run down the clock driving to and from the airport, and so we dream of extra days.

I moved to New York City because I didn't want to think about these things, God least of all. All I wanted was to listen carefully and master correct pronunciations. I wanted to take note of how the beautiful people held forks and chopsticks and admired certain books but never others, not unless they were trying to be funny, and I wanted to exploit the fact that my accent made me sound wealthier than I was and slightly smarter, too. Mainly I sought forgetfulness. For a long time I was happy to have outrun God, because he really wasn't going to be much help here.

On occasion the subject would come up. My evangelical background. *Wow*, flushed faces at parties leaned in to ask, *what was it like growing up with adults so hooked on fairy tales?* My ability to quickly change the subject eventually outstripped my embarrassment, but not before I had internalized every critique of what faith in God now signified in America: intolerance, sanctimony, tut-tutting over Hollywood and the welfare office, a yawning void where curiosity and compassion could be.

But when I felt led to a conversational place wherein I was expected to confirm that everyone who takes part in the rituals of organized religion drags their knuckles on their way to stoning the town slut, I would stop. I couldn't. That I would have to drop the word "soul" from my vocabulary I hadn't expected. Sometimes a day delivered snatches of the Sermon on the Mount and I pictured the sermon as my father might, with Jesus sounding suspiciously like Alan Rickman. Jesus is up on a hill, surrounded by supporters, sweat pooling in the smalls of their backs, sun glinting off distant low-slung roofs. Jesus clears his throat and speaks these demonstrably false lines about the world we actually live in:

Blessed are the poor in spirit: for theirs is the kingdom of heaven.
Blessed are they that mourn: for they shall be comforted.
Blessed are the meek: for they shall inherit the earth.
Blessed are they which do hunger and thirst after righteousness:
    for they
shall be filled.
Blessed are the merciful: for they shall obtain mercy.
Blessed are the pure in heart: for they shall see God.
Blessed are the peacemakers; for they shall be called the children
    of God.
Blessed are they which are persecuted for righteousness' sake:
for theirs is the kingdom of heaven.

Translation for people like my people: If you are humble, you will be rewarded. Turn the other cheek because vengeance is the Lord's. If you suffer, use it. The light shining from sincere faces will be hard to deny.

When my parents visit me in New York, we avoid these questions in an East Village bar. I take them to McSorley's on East Seventh Street because it's dark and has sawdust on the floor. There's always a man at the bar gesturing as if to gather everyone to his chest, loudly railing against the New England Patriots or Woody Allen's mixed output. McSorley's is a bar with some history, and I thought my dad would like the fact that he could hang a story off McSorley's, a story that started with a line like "It was the oldest bar in New York" and got more sentimental from there. My father tends to push the warm brown details so that every scenario sounds like an outtake from *A Christmas Carol*.

Outside we kiss hello along with a half hug—one cheek, one-armed. That we drink alcohol still feels like a special allowance. Both of my parents grew up with Baptist pastors for fathers. From a young age they were told that some activities might be acceptable to some believers (Catholics primarily), but as for them and their household, they would shun alcohol, playing cards, and the movies. When my parents decided as a young married couple, knocking around a small white clapboard house in Iowa, that beer, wine, and an occasional brandy & 7UP were okay in God's eyes, they hoped this small rebellion carried the hint of a more expansive righteousness. Open-mindedness, perhaps. Decades later, having a drink still feels like a decision to be a particular kind of person.

At McSorley's in the afternoon, the aroma of stale beer has seeped into the worn wood surfaces, into the backs of framed sepia prints, overpowering the smells of cooking oil and the diluted Pine-Sol used to mop the floors at night. That soaked-in beery scent is an ungentle reminder that alcohol enjoyment has its limits, so we allow ourselves some self-congratulation: moderation is not generally a problem for us, although, as my father once said of his father: "It's a good thing Wes never drank, or he never would have stopped. Those Baptists were like alcoholics. It's basically the same psychology."

Thanks be to God, my parents would say. *Thanks to my ability to take care of myself*, I would say. My father knows I choose to fill my time with people for whom Christianity is an outmoded concept, a vestigial tail that humanity would be better off losing. He knows most of my friends are of the opinion that the country would be better off without people who think like he does. His new status as a cultural relic bothers him. He finds it ironic that moral relativists temporarily misplace their relativism when talk turns to Jesus. He doesn't like how "evangelical" and "fundamentalist" are so often conflated in news reports and in opinion pieces, as if there were no shadows between them. It seems to him more evidence that the United States is becoming a post-Christian society like England and much of Europe before it. Used to be, he remembers, one didn't have to explain the contours of faith. Billy Graham appeared on prime time television. Everyone in this country, he remembered, knew what faith was for.

Now, 15 percent of Americans polled claim no religious preference, twice the number who declared themselves uninterested in God in 1990. The share of Americans who think religion "can answer all or most of today's problems" is 48 percent—a big number, sure, but a historic low.

When Amy and I were very young, the common childhood complaint that *x* was *not fair*, while never explicitly outlawed in our house, was well understood to be fruitless. "Life's not fair!" was always the response. We knew the story of Job and understood the moral to be the same: You believe your situation ought to improve, but God may have other ideas. To dwell on plans of your own devising was sinful.

So because my father cannot protest that the systemic devaluation of all he holds dear feels unfair to him, he watches Fox News, which says it for him. Just 60 percent of Americans identify as religious, last he heard, while the ranks of atheists swell.

My mother is quieter on the subject, as usual. When the chardonnay and mugs of foamy beer are placed in front of us she looks around the room and smiles. Her eyes rest on the spoils of our drifting afternoon—paper shopping bags and $10 probably-not-pashminas bought from a street vendor. Coats are draped over seat backs and we are careful not to kick up too much of the sawdust that blankets the floor.

"Oh, it's so nice to sit down," she says. We are careful not to talk about Amy.

"Remember when we saw Rudy Giuliani at the Columbus Day parade? That was fun."

Both my parents shook his hand; my mother snapped a photo. We also know we cannot discuss politics or religion, so conversation pivots to subjects that do not expose how different we've become. Technology is one such subject; none of us likes it much. My father is intensely suspicious of social media.

He is also suspicious of people who get paid to tell other people how much everyone ought to be enjoying these new gadgets and how effective they make you and your photogenic family.

"You know most people think technology is neutral," he says. "Morally neutral. They think that the means don't affect us. That the technology is just at our disposal, doing what we want it to do but nothing more. But technology always bends toward the dark side."

I had heard him say this before. It was another favorite theme. By "always" he meant *always* and by "dark side" he meant that any new technological whizbang would eventually be used to hurt people, whether it be TNT or the efficient delivery of asphyxiate gas to shower stalls. That the harm in some cases was self-inflicted, of the type-A-who-can't-put-down-his-BlackBerry kind, didn't matter to him. His thinking on this front was heavily influenced by Jacques Ellul, a professor of law and sociology at the University of Bordeaux and a French Reformed lay minister who wrote some thirty books on Protestant theological themes. My father had read Ellul's *The Technological Society* at the recommendation of an old mentor, and Ellul's general idea that technology took on a life of its own, essentially training users to adapt to it rather than the other way around, had taken firm root in my father's mind around the same time he began questioning what he was really doing with his life, which if we as a family had to pull out a calendar and point to exact dates, would all select 1987, our widely acknowledged Most Crappy Year.

Ellul was also highly suspicious of our culture's tendency to celebrate efficiency, and this, too, my father appreciated. Wishing someone Happy Birthday! on Facebook, for instance. *Why in the world would anyone do that?* my father wanted to know. Maybe wishing someone a Happy Birthday shouldn't be so simple. Perhaps some tasks shouldn't be relatively effortless, maybe true gifts involved sacrifice, and perhaps we shouldn't assume we'd won some victory over time whenever we accomplished something faster. Left unchecked, social media would land us in a Tower of Babel moment. We'd all be blue in the face from talking, pinging, communicating all the time, and we'd lose the ability to say the unsayable.

He took a sip of beer, wiped his lips. My father drinks slowly. Because his black eyebrows are heavy and his jaw square, people used to say he looked like Marlon Brando, and he did for a while, until Brando ballooned and my father stayed roughly the same size. Most of his hair—shiny black, straight as straw—fell out from the top of his head when he was twenty-one. He's bald on top in their wedding photo. Before he stopped wearing a toupee about ten years ago, he had gray hairs added to it annually to match increasingly salt-and-pepper sideburns. My mother had been hounding him for years to be bald and proud, and now that he is, she fixes her gaze on his now-shiny bald head and smiles a crinkle-eyed smile. She is proud of him, of her, of all this evidence of our collective . . . something. She'd always preferred practicalities while he preferred abstractions, but in this choice to go bald they found common ground.

"Did you read *Propaganda*?" he asks me. *Propaganda* was another one of Ellul's books that accompanied us from house to house during my childhood, and—pure coincidence—I had recently discovered that the publishing company I worked for still had the paperback in print. I mentioned this to my father via email.

I shook my head. I hadn't and didn't want to. I only kept a copy on the shelf as a reminder of things and people I'd left behind.

"*Propaganda* nails the mass media right to the wall," he says with some satisfaction.

I did not ask him how that premise—that the mass media deserved to be nailed to the wall—jibed with his earlier decision to spend nine years of our family's life using 500,000-kilowatt radio towers to spread the Gospel. I also failed to see how it squared with his enjoyment of Rush Limbaugh and Bill O'Reilly and Dennis Prager podcasts. He had started to send me links to *Wall Street Journal* articles, so clearly some media was fine, and media that supported his increasingly conservative politics was not part of the subset of mass media that deserved to be nailed to the wall.

I nodded and looked to my mother. She just didn't like all the stupid chain emails, she said. Some people just don't know when to stop, she said. Or not forward emails.

She twirled the stem of her wineglass so its contents swirled to the rim.

A waitress stopped by to ask if we wanted another round. We did not. The afternoon was getting tired.

What did they still want to see or do in the city, I asked. Maybe the Frick? The Strand Book Store? Did Mom still want to look for knockoff purses in Chinatown? We are either overwhelmed by choice or straining to stay within the narrow band of our shared interests, but all we've decided by the time the check arrives is that after they nap at the hotel and I do whatever it is I do, we'll reconvene for Indian food at 6:30.

Conflicting views over the appropriate size of the tip are negotiated through eyebrows and frowns. When my father visits the men's room, my mother tucks an additional $2 into the check holder. Her eyes are almond-shaped and her complexion heavy cream, and while individually her features are hard to fault, their total falls several marks shy of beautiful, or so she has believed. Her dimples all but shout a desire to please.

"I just love New York," she says. "It's so interesting. So fascinating. I can't believe how well you know your way around the city. So impressive. You just know where everything is."

Her compliments to New York and to me are sincere but I push them away.

"There's no need to be impressed." I shrug. "I've lived here for eight years."

"I know. But *still*," she says. "It's so neat. I'm so proud of you."

That Christian commentators over many centuries have asserted that cities, unlike the Garden of Eden or mountains, which confronted us with God's majesty, were constructed precisely to provide a workable alternative to God is the background we're speaking against. Neither of us need reference the notion because it's in our blood. Also understood between us is that my mother's embrace of New York is her tiny rebellion, her signal to herself and to me, and to anyone who may be watching, that she's really quite open-minded.

Earlier on in this brief visit to New York she sat at my kitchen table and turned the pages of the Sunday *New York Times*, flipping first, as was her habit, to the obituaries. "My goodness. They go on for pages. Look at all these clubs and . . . associations. Wow. New York is a very impressive place."

Because I had my head in the refrigerator I couldn't read her expression. But I knew she meant that the *Times* was a monument to success measured in terms that made her squirm, or that the newspaper somehow knew that she, its reader, had never graduated from college.

All that to say this is not a story of judgmental zealots thumping pulpits and demanding we all come to a reckoning with our shortcomings before a perfect God. This is not a story about pious blowhards whose unbending conviction alienated their children forever.

Mistakes were made, but not the ones popularly imagined.

Which is to say that the Christians I know best are brokenhearted.

Every week for years my father has received a phone call from the 718 area code. At least one, sometimes more. The caller is usually a gentleman from the Bronx trying to reach a nearby AIDS clinic. A few months after this first began happening, my father finally asked a caller how he got his number. Turned out his 1-800 number was a single digit off the AIDS clinic's number, and so easily misdialed. Instead of changing his number he kept answering the 718 wrong numbers, and, as he explained to me, every time it happens he pays the 3¢ and says a quick prayer for these men from the Bronx. I tried to suggest that he probably doesn't need that 1-800 number anymore because hardly anyone uses 1-800 numbers anymore given that cell phone plans typically cover long distance calls and so any implied cost savings extended toward existing clients or prospective clients is really meaningless, and besides, does he want clients who would hesitate before placing a long distance call they'd have to pay for?

He keeps the 1-800 number.

We emerge blinking from McSorley's and look around us. To eyes not accustomed to its bricks and grime, the East Village looks both more sinister and more glamorous than it does to those used to how its old brick buildings flaunt lived-in-ness. There are still pockets of youth and flash, but the real money has moved south and farther east.

I hail a cab for my parents. I start walking south. As the East Village transitions to the Lower East Side, class disparities among strangers on the street become starker. The Lower East Side is a jumble of skin tones, colors, and noise, litter-strewn and loud. Here one-hundred-year-old four-story tenements are quickly replaced by glass-fronted sixteen-story "luxury" apartment towers with glossy lobbies and earpieced doormen who grew up in housing projects six blocks away. But when you glimpse an idling Cadillac Escalade, you still think "drug dealer," as it wasn't that long ago that heroin addicts claimed these streets as their own.

Now the streets teem with still-beautiful bodies, giggles, European tourists and college kids and more kids from the projects, all wearing clothes from Forever 21, babies having babies, bummed cigarettes and hipsters and that guy, always that guy, who's just realized that he's the oldest guy at the nightclub.

They're all doing fine. They're all fine, and when I'm blocks away from my memories I can think out loud: if God exists, surely he does not care whether these kids believe in him. If God exists, surely he delights in them.

"Stories of pious children tend to be false," Flannery O'Connor once remarked, and I found this line in a book of essays and underlined it, because that was my experience. What I most remember feeling in the presence of God was bashfulness. When at age five I told my mother that I wanted to accept Jesus into my heart, she pulled me into her lap and we prayed. Afterward she sniffled and a glassiness in her eyes suggested she was near tears. *But isn't this what I'm supposed to do?* I wondered. Clean your plate, clean your room, love this idea we call God. I scrambled off her lap and ran to grab my swimsuit because we'd be spending the afternoon at the beach.

The register my father's voice takes on when describing their decision to leave jobs as a high school teacher (him) or something-or-other career track at JCPenney (my mother) and become overseas missionaries is textured like driveway gravel.

"There was a richness about that experience. We were thirty-three, thirty-four—" he pauses. After a beat, he swallows and begins again.

"Your mother and I were very unsophisticated people, and at the age of thirty-three and thirty-one we quit Minnesota and we quit everything traditional and bought a Volkswagen camper and took our two kids and ran off to the Caribbean. Then Europe. In many ways, that's pretty unconventional. I think if we had been more sophisticated, we wouldn't have taken such risks."

Unconventional.

Sophisticated.

These are dog whistles. Appeals to my sympathy. *You and me*, he's saying—*we are not so dissimilar after all. You may not appreciate me now, but you began here, with us. You crafted your life from materials we provided.* For years as a young adult I feared being Christian meant congratulating yourself on accomplishments of scant economic utility, like not complaining when you broke your hip. I was afraid being Christian equaled not knowing how the game was really played. He sensed these judgments in every terse email exchange.

At my apartment, a snapshot of Amy and me—1978—standing in the back door of a baby-blue-and-white Volkswagen camper. It's parked in my grandparents' dirt driveway underneath elm trees. Our family was about to leave Minnesota for a month of missions training in Florida. Strangely, our outfits match the Volkswagen. I do not think this was deliberate. Amy would have been nearly nine, me three. We're giggling.

It was late summer, so there must have been raspberries from my grandparents' garden, and worries that we'd stain our clothes. From memories acquired later I know that Marian enjoyed telling her granddaughters that she prayed for us every day, each of us girls by name. She clutched floral cotton handkerchiefs, shaking her fist for emphasis, which, with the handkerchief spilling out, her good posture, chin up, gave the proclamation a V-for-Victory flair. Raspberries for the road in an empty Cool Whip container. My mother wearing late-seventies sunglasses. Orville would have started his send-off prayer with "Heavenly Father" and asked for our safety and the safety of others traveling the interstates with us.

I imagine my father would have been mostly silent, glancing at his Casio watch, swallowing impatiently at the drawn-out goodbyes. I imagine if he ever voiced his desire to get the show on the road, that's what he would have muttered. *Let's get this show on the road.* But not for his sake. He would never want to imply that. For the sake of avoiding heavy traffic.

On the third day of traveling we reached Boca Raton. Amy frowned as the camper pulled into the paved driveway of the Bibletown Community Church and Conference Center because Bibletown was not, contrary to her hopes, an open-air museum that simulated everyday life in ancient times. It was a modern building ringed by cement, closely cropped grass, and palm trees. Adults here studied fundraising techniques and how to handle culture shock while kids played in the pool under the watchful eye of volunteer teenagers who, after much prayer, had determined that serving as lifeguard for the children of future missionaries would consecrate their summer vacation.

One long day Amy decided it would be fun to jump off the diving board backward. She came within an inch of scraping skin off her nose and landed in the pool with limbs splayed awkwardly. The bad splash prompted every adult witness to scramble out of lounge chairs in anticipation of having to pull a dead girl from the water, and the sixteen-year-old lifeguard to shed hiccupy near-miss tears once Amy was safely back poolside, flinging water drops from her face with shaking fingers. She was *fine*, Amy insisted. *Everybody stop making a fuss.*

Our second week in Florida: Disney World. For one last blast of U.S.A., our father said. Midday it started pouring rain so Mom ducked into the nearest souvenir shop and returned with two blue Magic Kingdom beach towels.

"That doesn't make any sense," Amy said. Our mother began draping a blue towel over Amy's skinny head and shoulders, urging us to huddle closer. Amy and I looked around at other kids—resplendent in hooded Disney rain gear. Drops ran off the slick edges of pink Cinderella rain ponchos and it appeared these rain poncho owners were having much, much more fun.

"But it's *raining*. Mom! Why didn't you get us rain ponchos?"

"I got towels because rain ponchos won't really be needed on Bonaire. But we will probably never have enough beach towels, you know?"

Within five minutes the downpour had slackened into drips and we ventured out from under the awning a little wiser.

Much, much later, over white wine and Marlboro Lights, Amy would pinpoint the pink Cinderella rain poncho hour as a pivotal moment of her awakening.

"That's when I knew we were poor," she said. She stamped out her Marlboro Light and lit another one.

We will keep having this conversation, Amy and I. According to this version of our story, excessive and poorly executed love of God had cheated us out of futures we deserved. We would be secular with a vengeance.

✦

When family myths break, by which I mean stop working, it helps to place disparate memories in some semblance of order. The thing is, to remember any event correctly, you have to have noticed it in the first place. This noticing sensation then travels to your brain's hippocampus, where it is encoded. When we say we experienced something, that's what we're talking about, this bundle of sensations and perceptions being packaged by the hippocampus. Our hippocampus gathers these packages and weighs them and decides which ones are important enough to become long-term memories. When we remember a thing, our hippocampus pulls these packages out of storage and attaches words to them. Every time we do this, that memory becomes stronger. The rest lapses into shadow. Memories rarely hauled out of storage become harder and harder to find. Some are manufactured from photographs and assumptions borrowed from other memories.

Try remembering, too, when you don't see your relatives that often. The routine hauling out of memories, shaping and refining them against one another's versions of what happened, is not routine for someone like you. Especially when you're afraid to remember because who you are is not something you're sure you want to know.

After years of feeling like an alien I knew I had fully reassimilated into American culture when I overheard myself defending "Have a nice day." A visiting Londoner was intent on informing me it was *urghhh too too saccharine* and *stupid*. I protested that the practice was harmless, and in any event better than wishing someone ill—a common enough occurrence in any culture. What I failed to realize then is that I wasn't just talking about America, and I wasn't only thinking of social pleasantries. I was defending my evangelists. I heard echoes of my mother, my grandmother, church ladies everywhere singing *This is the day that the Lord has made; Let us rejoice and be glad in it.*

BONAIRE

In a letter dated December 8, 1978, my mother described the weather patterns inside our new house on Bonaire, Netherlands Antilles, fifty miles off the Venezuelan coast:

> Just as I began typing this, the rain started pouring down . . . Or sideways, I guess, —the wind really blows sometimes and the rain can be felt on the opposite side of the room from the windows!! It usually doesn't last more than a few minutes, then the sunshine is out again—but this will happen about 10 times a day.

The skinny bare legs, wet knees, giggles, the darkening skies and high rolling clouds, the being careful not to slip on wet tile. I remember that room, and the brief innocence of not belonging but not minding. The switching on the car radio and hearing, over static and car horns and sweaty thigh *thwocks* on hot upholstery, the voices of people who sat next to you at church.

✦

The thirty families working for Trans World Radio were distinguished from the island's other whites mainly by wardrobe. People who worked for Royal Dutch Shell or shipping companies did not make do with donated or secondhand clothes. Among one another, Bonaire's missionaries joked of looking like missionaries—frumpy, for the most part, and pasty. References to the states they called home were made almost apologetically. Everything past was staging ground.

Trans World Radio's red-and-white transmitters were by far the tallest structures on the island. The attraction Bonaire held for TWR's founders was mainly due to its flatness and salt. Bonaire had piles of salt, and a flat, salty strip of land, surrounded by seawater on all sides, offered excellent conductivity for radio signals, so that when atmospheric conditions were right, you could hear TWR Bonaire's programs on shortwave radio in Canada and on down to Argentina and shacks deep in the Amazon jungle. The engineers working the transmitter came from Tennessee or the Carolinas or Michigan and wore leather tool belts and bit their nails while contemplating engine parts. God and the rightness of His rules for living were a foregone conclusion. They were just seeing to the mechanics but they took the mechanics seriously. Studio workers on the second shift queued up *Radio Today*, whose intended audience was waking up in India. When TWR Bonaire was granted the use of AM 800, it was taken as further evidence of God's blessing.

Sometimes, sleepless and barefoot in white nightgowns, we visited Dad at work. He'd be keeping watch over the console, listening for any worrying clanks in the twin forty-five-ton, sixteen-cylinder Alco diesel engines, large as locomotives, used to generate the 3.2 million watts of electricity needed to send the signals as far as they were intended to go. His shift partners—named Chuck or Bruce or Tim—all kept a polite distance as Amy and I whispered and stifled the urge to push mysterious buttons.

Chuck Roswell, toothpicked and toolbelted, kept a stash of fluorescent lightbulbs by the table by the exit leading out to where the towers towered. When the Alco engines ran at full power, all you had to do was walk outside into the tar-pitch dark, out toward the towers, and stretch out your arm to hold the bulb aloft in the air. There was enough ambient electricity to make it glow, strong and insistent.

"Don't even need a flashlight," Chuck would grin. Best of all was the circular bulb. That way you could give yourself a halo.

In my mother's next letter to her parents:

> Yesterday and last night our electricity was on & off—mostly off—about 5xs. —And when it goes off you have to unplug everything because of the surge when it comes back on—Refrig. + freezer are hurt the most by it—it really wrecks the motor. —Anyway, all of Bonaire was without power from 2PM–10PM last night. It gets dark here now about 6:30. Water is turned off quite often, too—& never any explanation as to why!

My parents decided that this missing explanation was a spiritual challenge. To wonder but not get satisfying answers was part of what we were being called to do. Bugs and how we respond to them either reflected God's grace or did not.

> The Bonairians don't get upset because that's all they know—but we always say or think that it's not that way back home— TWR has their own power so they aren't affected.

Subtext for any people at home worried about how we were going to pull this stunt off: don't worry that money you've donated to the cause is going to waste because Antilleans can't reliably keep the lights on.

✦

That a sense of enchantment would be needed became clearer in time. I was three years old and had no clear conception of God but figured he was related to George Washington, who was also aged and on the dollar bill. (Neither, tellingly, was referenced on Bonairian money, and perhaps that explained our presence on the island.) Upon arrival at the airport—white Americans' suitcases warrant closer inspection. Upon being given a tour of our first island home—we forgot to pack a fan. Could we buy one on the island? No. How? We'd have to write to someone in the States and request they send one. The house was mustard yellow, single story, and had no bathtub. We would have to check the shower stall for scorpions before stepping in because they liked damp spaces. So, too, our shoes before putting them on. ("Pick them up and look inside and give them a good shake.") Close the outside gate or the wild goats would make themselves at home and eat everything, especially red things, like hibiscus flowers. There's no telling when or if the flowers would grow back. And the water temperature varied by time of day because all pipes ran above ground, not below, *the way it was back home.* So in the early mornings water ran cold and by noon it was hot; by one p.m. it scalded.

But our animating idea acquired force over time. Our job on this earth was to imagine beyond the immediate facts at hand. You had to think twice because humility was attractive, and not trusting your first reactions was one way of being humble, and perhaps the most important. Using different words helped, too. The Bonaire word for big cockroaches was *kakalakas*, for instance. Large tropical cockroaches seemed better, possibly beautiful, when graced with a name like *kakalaka*. That people had figured this out was reason enough for gratitude.

The real task for our family emerged at the edges of my ability to comprehend it: Dad's at the transmitter site, and Mom, Amy, and Megan are squinting into the sun on the way to Kralendijk's supermarket. A man we'd seen loitering around on earlier trips downtown half stumbles, half runs over. His clothes are filthy. He smells of sweat and dog treats.

He bends down to pick me up and yanks on a blond pigtail so my head bobbles.

My mother yelps and lunges for my arm.

"*Mom*," Amy says.

"*Ow*," I say.

"*Mom*," Amy repeats.

"Hi," my mother says. "Hello." She forces her face into an expression that says *Please release my child*, and he does. I stuff my feet back into my sandals as he fishes around in his pants pocket. Three wrapped candies along with sand and lint are extended with trembling hand.

"Thank you," my mother says. "Oh, thank you so much. That's so nice."

On subsequent trips to the supermarket, I kept a firm grip on my mother's skirt. Any darkened aisle might have contained him, so I scanned every aisle under the flickering fluorescent lights, hoping for invisibility sometimes and other times for his removal from the face of the earth. My mother tried to assure me there was nothing to be afraid of because the man was only trying to be friendly. Obviously he wasn't too good at it yet, but this was our job, as representatives of Christ's love. To accept wrapped candy with gladness, because if we didn't, who knows what or who would be lost forever.

At breakfast we poured reconstituted powdered milk over stale cereal, stirred the cereal, and watched and waited for dead ants to float to the top. Then I scooped the ants out with my spoon and deposited them on the tabletop and proceeded to eat the cereal, any memory of how cereal eating was supposed to commence already lost to me. *Think of it this way*, my mother added, for good measure, because I don't remember protesting: the reason our cereal bowl contained dead ants was because the cereal box had probably lingered on a loading dock in Miami for weeks, waiting for customs clearance, and that was interesting, right? To eat cereal that had been in Miami? Dead ants were wiped up with a kitchen sink sponge and swirled down the drain, back out to sea.

✦

We had been led here. That is the missionary's position. Jimmy Carter had made a big deal in his 1976 campaign—1976, the year of the evangelical, according to *Newsweek*—about how decadence threatened the integrity of the American family. But to be Christian at Trinity Lutheran Church of Minnehaha Falls in 1978 Minneapolis was to have the whole world on your mind. The church had sent missionaries to Bangladesh, Bolivia, Ecuador, India, Kenya, Madagascar, Nepal, New Guinea, Pakistan, Peru, South Africa, and Tanzania. Their names and host countries were recited aloud at every Sunday worship service. Pastor Johansson told stories of hot dangerous days in the horn of Africa, working at Radio Voice of the Gospel in Addis Ababa, Ethiopia. The station had been granted its operating license by Emperor Haile Selassie, rumored to like Lutheran evangelicals, before being shut down by Marxists in 1973.*

Meeting Pastor Johansson seemed accidental at first. My father had stormed out postargument with my mother for a head-clearing walk. (They disagreed on how much a Monopoly winner should gloat.) Ten minutes later he found himself locked out of the house, and so returned to the sidewalk, hands stuffed in pockets, muttering into the cold. Within two and a half blocks was Trinity Lutheran, so he ducked in and took a seat toward the back to warm up. During the recessional Pastor Johansson, stately in liturgical robes, glimpsed my father, slumped and scowling. He stopped and said, "You look like you need a friend."

They became confidants. Weekly conversations in the fifteen minutes before the first service each Sunday revealed that

---

*Swedish Lutherans in Ethiopia—there's a photo, I later discovered, of a Ms. Anna-Lena Jansson dressed in traditional Swedish costume, standing primly next to Crown Prince Asfa Wossen, dressed in whatever Ethiopian royal highnesses wore in the 1920s, on the occasion of the opening of Ms. Jansson's Girls' School, or Bible True Friends School for Girls. Ms. Jansson, pioneering as she was, wasn't an original. The first Swedish evangelical mission in Ethiopia dated back to 1904 and the arrival of a certain Karl Cederquist, who persuaded many of his countrymen to join him.

Pastor Johansson used words like "paradox." For my father it was thrilling to say something sideways to his actual meaning—because his actual meanings frightened him sometimes—and still be understood. He could say, for instance, "I'm having a rough week at school," and Pastor Johansson heard clearly the more insistent hungers burbling below. Out in the sanctuary—palpable excitement. Standing room only. Young men in jeans seated on the steps to the altar, soaking in acceptance.

My parents first heard of TWR while watching Billy Graham's *Hour of Decision* one night. Like the BBC or Voice of America, but sanctified. My father took this idea of missionary radio to Pastor Johansson. Was he being called to do this? he asked. Pastor Johansson told him he didn't object to the term "calling" per se, but one should be careful. How would you know that that feeling was a calling? It could be indigestion.

Still, Pastor Johansson said, remain open to the mystery.

"View it as an adventure," he said. Besides, growing up overseas would be great for the kids.

Then: consider the Gospel account of Jesus's baptism. Mark, chapter 1, opens with a wild-eyed John the Baptist, Jesus's cousin, clothes made of camel's hair, diet of locusts and honey, wandering the desert. People left their sweltering cities and traveled to John, swearing to throw off their soft, indulgent lives and be baptized in the Jordan River. Then Jesus himself came to be baptized by John, and *just as Jesus was coming up out of the water, he saw heaven being torn open and the Spirit descending on him like a dove. And a voice came from heaven: "You are my Son, whom I love; with you I am well pleased."* The Gospel of Matthew version of the story included a conversation between John the Baptist and Jesus as they stood on the riverbank, a conversation in which John effectively says, *Whoa, cousin, why should I baptize you?* Jesus tells John to do it already.

Here's the thing, Pastor Johansson continued: Most people were afraid of strong feeling. They were like John at this moment. They tried to talk us out of our epiphanies. When we wanted to devote ourselves wholeheartedly to a task, these people would say, *Come now. Be sensible. Are you sure?* And that was the fundamental confrontation for all of us: between well-meaning people who sought to shelter us, and Jesus, who set us free.*

✦

The founder of Trans World Radio, Dr. Paul Freed, believed that randomness was a fiction—for certain types of people. If a person met regularly in prayer with the Lord and pleaded for the Lord's guidance, then whatever opportunities came before him or her could not be chalked up to happenstance. In fact, it was presumptuous to say "I *happened* to" do something, or "I *happened* to meet" so-and-so, or "By *chance*" we wound up doing this or that, because how, really, could one know?

"If you are in a particular spot and you run into a certain person," he wrote in *Towers to Eternity*, his account of TWR's early years, "if you even walk to the store or take a trip, and all of these things are done with your heart open to the Lord, must you not then assume that He is directing you in the path of His will?"

Freed saw evidence for how nothing *just happened* to God-

---

*My father broke the news to Wes over the phone. He thought the Billy Graham connection would seal Wes's approval. It didn't.

"You're going to quit your job?" Wes asked. "Why would you want to do that?"

Vivian's cooing usually made the meaning of her words subservient to the sound. His mother's "How are you" typically said *Woe is me* and sometimes *I'm not sure how to respond to what's happening here but it would be nicer if everyone just got along.* On this call it said both.

After hanging up my father vacillated between two interpretations of Wes's reaction. Either Wes was not fully sincere in his faith (because if he were, presumably he'd be glad at this news) or Wes was a limited man. His was your basic I-don't-like-spicy-foods reaction, but with subtle emotional kneecapping. Or Wes's reasoning was that if you went someplace unknown, you were begging for unknown things to happen to you. Showing yourself was daring the world to call your bluff. Hunker down instead.

As he thought longer, he arrived at a fourth possible interpretation. Wes had always parented herky-jerkily. His love involved shielding the beloved from the burden of developing the courage of their convictions. Make decisions for them! It shows you care!

The last possible interpretation arrived in my father's mind fully formed and it was the worst of all. Perhaps Wes started jawing about jobs, job security, etc., because he had no confidence in his son's abilities. This possibility stung.

fearing people in the birth of TWR's first transmitter, in Monte Carlo. Freed first began entertaining the idea of a radio network broadcasting steady encouragement to Christian believers without regular access to a community of faith while he was traveling through Spain in the fifties. He observed how Franco's restrictive excesses pressed on Protestant evangelicals. He found a spot across the Strait of Gibraltar from which to experiment. The Voice of Tangier was a low-powered station run on a shoestring budget, but the experience emboldened him to think bigger.

Finding a site from which to broadcast religious programming on the European mainland proved more difficult. Private concerns could not buy time on European airwaves for any price. But a solution emerged from an unlikely place. Monaco, den of glossy iniquity, casino gambling, and cocktails, would play host. The reason was not sympathy for Freed's cause. The Monaco authorities were agnostics, as far as he could tell, but agnostics willing to discuss price, which is more than could be said for the government-run media concerns elsewhere in Europe. That, and they happened to have, atop Mount Agel, the shell of a never-finished radio station built by the Nazis and subsequently abandoned at the end of World War II.

In April 1959, Freed and his advisers went into a meeting prepared to offer $50,000. Mr. Bosio of Radio Monte Carlo said that ten times that number sounded about right, and that the board of directors would also want TWR to cover the cost of installing an antenna system and new 100,000-watt transmitter, but in any event the $500,000 could be broken into six payments staggered over two years.

Freed agreed to sign a contract in one month's time knowing he didn't have the money or obvious means of getting it. Freed wondered if he'd lost his mind. Then some evangelical revivalists he had met on a recent trip to Oslo felt led to drop $83,000 into the TWR bank account, which took care of the inaugural payment. When the second payment came due, Freed was $13,000 short. Secretary knocks on his office door that very morning, waving a letter opener and a $5,000 check. At 11:30 a.m. he announces he's leaving for the bank. On the street he runs into a staffer returning from the post office. Another envelope, another $5,000 check.

"How are things coming along?" the president of the Chatham Trust Company asks Freed as he steps into his office. *Very well*, Freed says. The bank president reminds him he's still $13,000 short.

"Three thousand," Freed corrects.

The phone rings. It's Western Union, informing Chatham Trust of an incoming deposit of $3,000 for the TWR account.

No one knows what to say.

"Well, I know who sent it," Freed finally says. "God sent it!"

"Who did you say?"

"God sent it."

The bank president squints, shakes his head. *Sorry. Didn't quite hear you. What was the man's name?*

Freed repeats himself, more slowly now. *Al-migh-ty God sent it.*

✦

My father set his alarm for 2:30 a.m. so he could dress and splash water on his face, hop on his moped to get to work by 3:00. Shifts began with the switching on of machines: start up the Alco engines, check the oil, listen for any unusual clanks, engage the twin turbines. Once the turbines were churning out enough electricity, he or his shift partner hit the switch that let electricity flow to the radio towers. At 3:25 the junior transmitter operator dialed the studio technician in his lonely but air-conditioned booth to say that they were ready to go on air. First up was the Bonaire national anthem.

Later: "I didn't realize Bonaire had a national anthem," I say when my father narrates this morning routine to me. "Oh yes," he says. Of course a rinky-dink island would insist on a national anthem. Smaller you are, the more you stand on ceremony.

The day's first full program was in Portuguese, because in the backwoods of Brazil it was already 4:30 a.m. and people would be getting ready for work—that is, the people who really worked for a living, however meager. At 5:00 a.m. TWR switched to Spanish, and at 7:15 the day's first English-language programming began.

One day my father was woken up at 3:02 a.m. by a phone call. It was Chuck Roswell. Two people had to be on-site before the Alco engines could be turned on—those were the rules. As my father wasn't there, Chuck did not turn them on, and so unless my father could materialize at the transmitter fairly immediately, TWR Bonaire would be late getting on air that morning. Upon his bed-headed late arrival his punishment came in the form of the unspoken suggestion that he loved God a little less than people who came to work reliably on time did.

He began praying that his talents would be used more effectively. He understood that starting on the graveyard shift was the norm. All earthly organizations had hierarchies and he was the new guy and thus on the bottom. He would have to be patient and learn what he could in the process.

During long hours when there was little to do other than be there should something break, he wrote letters to his parents:

I am still working the 3 am–11 am transmitter shift. I am also doing some afternoon newscasts, probably starting next week— We are busy, but happy— We pray daily for God's grace for our family—

In a later letter I would like to talk to you about will and finances. Maybe a tape— My tape recorder should be here soon and we can exchange tapes. If you or any one asks, "What can we do?" Magazines + Books would be helpful. —I miss Time + Newsweek, Karen misses Good Housekeeping etc. A subscription would be nice— Have to get back to work— More later.

Love, Stan

In the note sent to supporters—titled "Hustads Arrive on Bonaire" and dated September 1978—he follows standard missionary prayer letter formula:

1. A brief summary of the situation on the ground: *At 12:12 AM on August 9th, after a 16-hour day of airplanes and airports at Newark, Miami, and Curaçao; Stan, Karen, Amy, and Meg arrived on Bonaire, Netherlands Antilles. We were welcomed by members of the TWR staff and taken to a temporary home pending the arrival of our home-making equipment so that we can then take up permanent residence.*

2. Thanks to God: *We thank the Lord for a safe trip and for the opportunity to finally begin our long anticipated ministry with Trans World Radio.*

3. Prayer requests: *We continue to earnestly seek your prayer support for us personally and for our ministry. We know that this is where God wants us and we pray that He will sharpen our spiritual lives and technical skills so that we will be effective instruments in His service.*

Later that month, his letter displays a growing preoccupation with how to approach things like petty theft and missing appliances in a fashion befitting someone whose job title announced seriousness about God:

Dear Mom + Dad—

I really don't know how long ago it was since I last wrote. I don't really remember everything that I may have told you— We appreciate your letters. I hope you will understand if we cannot always respond or write as soon as you would like us to. We do appreciate mail— We don't get very much!! People aren't writing yet—

We have had some good & bad experiences here. The bad one was that during church someone broke into the wash house where we were staying and stole all of our snorkeling equipment. Over $100 worth— You really need it for recreation on Bonaire— We went out & bought some more, but that was unpleasant. We have moved into what will be our permanent home but the missionary family that lived here has just not gotten their things out of storerooms & the yard is full of their junk. They are either thoughtless or inconsiderate as it has been 6 weeks since they were to be out— We have asked them but they don't get around to it. I have to have grace to know how to handle it— It is well said that often the biggest problems that missionaries face are other missionaries. Pray for us in these matters. We are hopefully going to get our appliances & bed soon. They have been traced down and will be here soon, we hope—

A missionary really begins to love his efficiency when things are so unsettled— It is just a small part, but we trust that God will honor our small efforts— We are going to like Bonaire— We have that feeling now & we PTL for it. We can be happy here— It is different— It has some hassles but we like the beautiful water and climate, though sometimes it is really hot, and we can live, grow & function as a family—

Love + Prayer
Stan

PTL = Praise the Lord. Those of us without jobs woke up warm in the middle of the night with sweaty necks and sweaty foreheads. Amy discovered that flipping the pillow over so that you could rest your head on the relatively cool side underneath brought enough relief to get you back to sleep. On nights the fan wasn't enough to dispel the heat, our mother invited us to get up and stuff sleepy feet into sandals.

Once parked we clambered out of the Volkswagen camper. The plan was to walk up and down Far Beach, only going so far as we could see by the light of the Volkswagen camper's headlights. We handed Mom our sandals and she dangled them off long fingers and spoke of the seashells we would find come daylight, how to see animal shapes in driftwood. It would be don't-even-glance-at-the-clock late by the time we brushed off our feet before being tucked back in.

Amy and I fretted about getting sand in the bed.

"We'll survive," my mother said. Kisses on foreheads, noses, ears before shutting off the light.

✦

ELLUL What was the role of the Christian? He felt it was easily summarized. Imagine God speaking here:

1. You are the salt of the earth.
2. You are the light of the world.
3. I send you forth as sheep in the midst of wolves.

Why salt? The Christian helped preserve the world. Light? Light eliminates darkness. Sheep in the midst of wolves? Much more difficult. You see, Ellul continued, in *the world* everybody wanted to be a wolf. It seemed more fun. In the world, i.e., outside God's kingdom, no one is called to play the part of a sheep. Trouble was, the world needed creatures that were willing to sacrifice themselves, just as Jesus Christ submitted himself to death on the cross.

That is why it is essential, Ellul maintained, that Christians be careful not to be wolves in the spiritual sense—that is, people who try to dominate others. "Christians ought to accept the domination of other people, and offer daily the sacrifice of their lives, which is united with the sacrifice of Jesus Christ." Nor were these metaphors, a pretty way of speaking. "On the contrary, these expressions denote a stark reality, from which it is impossible to escape." Our vulnerability would point people to God, and remind them in some still, small way of alternatives.

✦

Ruby Bock, the wife of the man tasked with serving as pastor to TWR's staff, asked my mother what church we attended back in the States. We were standing on the beach in bright sunlight, scraping hair away from our eyes, but not Mrs. Bock, whose silver hair did not move.

What church? "Trinity Lutheran" was not a good answer.

"I don't know how you can consider yourself a Christian when you go to a Lutheran church," Mrs. Bock replied.

Mrs. Bock was herself Southern Baptist. Lifestyle regulations popped up in casual conversations, usually after Sunday morning church services, invariably spoken in wind chime cadences. Jackie Ringema touched my mother on the elbow and pulled her into the side aisle of the TWR sanctuary, a boxlike warehouse building with a floor of poured cement, off-white cinder block walls, and very little adornment. *Maybe*, Jackie smiled sweetly, *you know, just maybe it would be helpful to you as a family to know a little more about the unofficial dress code for TWR people down here.* Jackie was plump and held her left forearm and hand protectively over her stomach as she spoke. It seemed necessary to open one's eyes wide during conversations like this because it would be all too easy to miss a clue. Big metal box fans kept the air moving and voices straining to be heard.

"Also," Jackie said. "We wear panty hose. In church."

"Ahuh," my mother nodded.

"Well, at least the women do!" and everyone giggled at this sudden dalliance into the risqué. "And sundresses are okay but the shoulder straps really need to be wider than—"

My mother was wearing spaghetti straps. "Okay. How wide?"

"At least two inches."

Smiles smiles smiles. *Of course.*

The next Sunday, Amy emerged from Sunday school class blinking furious tears away. She was initially reluctant to explain why she was crying, but with plenty of encouragement confessed that the Sunday school teacher had informed her *in front of the whole class* that it would be much better (for everyone?) if Amy would stop bringing the Good News Bible to Sunday school class and bring the King James version. They used the King James Bible in class because, the teacher explained, that was the translation Jesus's own disciples had used. My father considered challenging this but decided not to; the Sunday school teacher was not too bright, and there was nothing to be gained by embarrassing her.

But though we felt aslant of the prevailing missionary habits, we quickly became accustomed to the sound of our thighs unsticking from gunmetal folding chairs, coughs, and throat clearings muffled by heat and the whir of the fans. Amy knew and I was told that in the States, some children were released into "Children's Church" before the sermon started and didn't have to endure twenty-minute sermons on topics that didn't concern any moral choices children typically face. But not so here on the mission field, because missionary children represented a stronger strain of Christianity. We were better equipped for boredom, and this capacity for sitting through a sermon and then Sunday school was proof of our strong character. We were not missionary kids but MKs. We had acronym status and though none of us knew what an acronym was, we sensed its import: you, person called by an acronym, you are special. On the hottest Sundays we folded church bulletins into accordion fans and felt creative, too. Sunday school songs encouraged us to think of ourselves as bursting with promise "with a capital *P*." We were great big bundles of po-ten-ti-al-i-ty. If we learned how to listen for God's voice, we could be anything God wanted us to be. *Anything God wants me to be!* repeated at every verse's end.

In a letter to my father's parents, my mother mentioned offhand that Pastor Bock was under the impression that he went to Northern Seminary at the same time Wes did, back in the early forties. Maybe they knew each other. "We really appreciate him," she wrote. This was a lie, but nonetheless an accurate reflection of what she wanted to see in her heart. She figured that this made it okay, and that if she told herself she was grateful for the Bocks often enough, gratitude would follow.

✦

Many programs TWR aired were produced in the States but were thought to have potentially greater appeal overseas. The principle animating these programs was the universality of broken lives. Everyone knew a drunk uncle. Boys with knife wounds on their cheeks. Men called Slick-Fingers Sammy and others "not exactly sober." If your life had not panned out—if *you* had not panned out—consider Jesus, because the universe had a beating heart and through it pumped amazing grace whose purpose was to render meaningless the meagerness of your life achievements to date. The most popular such program was *Unshackled*.

Unshackled was the brainchild of a native New Yorker who moved to Chicago as an engineer with Consolidated Edison Company. Harry Saulnier began his ministry by volunteering at the Pacific Garden Mission, a soup kitchen and flophouse founded by the evangelist Dwight L. Moody and named after the building's previous tenant, the Pacific Beer Garden. To have a Christian charity named after a notorious bar was a joke—a joke that testified to God's ability to make all things new.

Saulnier began producing a fifteen-minute radio program called *Doorway to Heaven* but quickly felt it fell short of the medium's potential. If he could only successfully mimic the popular radio drama format, Saulnier believed they might really pull heartstrings. Enter a man at the Moody Bible Institute with a knack for script writing, and Saulnier soon convinced radio station WGN to air a new and improved show about the lurid *before*s leading up to moments of conversion. The show's title was gifted by a former navy man who breathlessly explained that the word "shackled" began every radio call at sea, while "unshackled" ended it. Unshackled: a three-syllable summary of life in Christ. *For you were called to freedom*, the Bible promised. They understood this to mean that once a man had accepted Jesus as his savior, he could no longer fairly be identified with past mistakes.

Organ music introduced the story, then first-person narration from a man whose appetites nearly ruined him:

> "The very best I could do was ten thousand, five hundred," I told him. "If you can't go the extra, maybe I can help you."
>
> "Don't worry, Lew," he said. "I can swing it, I think. It's such a nice little house. Thank you, Son."
>
> After I helped him move, being very careful not to scratch his favorite easy chair, I took his check, cashed it and paid the owner his eighty-five hundred dollars. Then I counted my change—about two thousand dollars—and pocketed it . . .
>
> From then on, deals seemed to come natural to me.

What went without saying is that cons and creeps often not only behaved badly but prided themselves on doing so. The responsibility of responding to the listener letters *Unshackled* generated fell to TWR staffers without specific work assignments. Wives, mainly. People who could respond without blinking.

> I made London my next stop and hooked up with Madam Bernice Deploya, a short, plump East Indian "clairvoyant and mystic" from the Bronx. She and I had most of our trouble over watches and stickpins I lifted from the clientele.
>
> When I was through with that job, I left for New York City and finally Chicago in 1924. My particular trade was a little slow that year, but I heard that street corner hawking was good on Skid Row.

How to wean people from the imaginary joys of behaving badly? In *Unshackled* they descend into dark nights of the soul, take whiskey as cough medicine, watch cockroaches play on the walls. They argue with every circumstance and everybody. They meet someone who proposes Jesus, and they argue some more. ("Jesus? Never heard such rot in my life. Makes me mad." "Oh yeah? You've been blasting and cursing God for years. God won't take it forever." Answer: "He sure will. He has to." Reply: "He does not." Answer: "But he does, because he doesn't exist.")

Then somehow, before the half hour was over, the narrator accepted his unworthiness and in this defeat finds grace. Peace ensues. He chooses God and the rest takes care of itself.

✦

Amy caught on quickly to the new sounds we needed to make. Every day she came home from St. Bernardus her tongue could form another new Dutch word, and she demonstrated the sharp *k*'s, taut *u*'s, and raspy *g*'s that seemed to necessitate phlegm buildup at the back of the throat. Sometimes her teacher smoked in the classroom, which worried her. During recess, more important, the kids switched to Papiamento, the language they spoke at home. Why they needed two languages she couldn't quite grasp but figured it made keeping secrets easier.

That she was going to St. Bernardus and not the island's other elementary school was an unusual choice by TWR standards. Only the Miller family had also opted for this Catholic school. No one denied that St. Bernardus was the better school—the teachers were better, the central Kralendijk location more convenient, the students less rowdy. But it also could not be denied that whereas the other school was secular, St. Bernardus was Catholic. Many TWR parents worried that being forced to recite Hail Marys every morning would theologically confuse their kids. It was all right to respect Mary, for she was Jesus's mother. But to revere her too greatly was a mistake.

Amy decided she could mouth along with the Hail Marys and not actually speak them, and no one would notice. She also did not mind being the only white girl in her class. She took the stares of her classmates and replied with smiles. When she spoke, she spoke with confidence that people would be patient with her still-wobbly Dutch syntax. *Praise the Lord that Amy is adjusting so well!* my mother wrote in letters home. Evidence that God could be trusted was everywhere.

I sat at the kitchen table in the hour before picking Amy up from school and watched as my mother filled the yellow mission-provided flamingo stationery with blue ballpoint cursive reports on how we were doing.

"What are those?" I asked.

"Exclamation points," she said.

"What are those for?"

"They're for changing the tone."

"The tone?"

"Remember when we talked about tone of voice? *How* you say something is important, not just the words you're using. It let's people know you're happy, or very serious, or mean and angry."

"Why do you put them—" "These exclamation points mean we're happy. We're very happy."

The appearance of skin rashes did little to dampen this enthusiasm. "Impetigo" sounded exciting but it itched. Dr. Welvaart and other missionary moms said it was just part of island life—the sun, salt, heat was hard on young skin, and impetigo was highly contagious, so most Bonaire kids had either just recovered from it or were about to suffer itchy blisters on their butts and thighs soon. Recommended treatment involved solutions of gentian violet, which unlike most medicines was consistently available at the island's sole *botika*. One capful of gentian violet per bucketful of water. Place the bucket on the floor of the shower and sit your kid naked in it for ten minutes before bedtime. We tried to inflect *gentian violet* with the same whispery glamor, we hoped, used to refer to sparkly floor-length gowns or chocolate cigarettes from the airport gift shop.

✦

Sometimes men in short-sleeved uniforms would turn off their English. They'd quote a figure and when asked why so high shrugged *Sorry, Miss* and stared over shoulders toward the Tia Maria advertisement on the far wall until wallets were extracted from pockets and prices paid. A person could be detained at customs for a half hour while they removed everything from your suitcase and put it back again. Searching for drugs was the rumored reason. Once in the belly of Amy's teddy bear, which had to be sewn up afterward. We pretended it had hernia surgery.

I knew that the reason for this was our privilege. I had a dimmer sense that people often did things simply because they could, and it was almost too much to ask someone to abstain from doing something they were capable of.

How to move among the locals? My father had determined that the best way to think about our position on the island was as guests, which meant quiet when going about day-to-day business, mainly, but had a few other practical considerations: no special outfit (missionary clothes were modest enough not to spark envy or disapproval), no door-to-door proselytizing (that wasn't what TWR did), and consistent politeness.

Mainly it meant allowing the people who needed to push you around a little to do so. Let your white American privilege be offset by suffering small moments. Dr. Welvaart saw white patients and animals on certain afternoons only. The lady who sold eggs out of her home allocated her customers specific hours. If you, white person, showed up at 2:50 and your scheduled time was 3:00 p.m., you waited. She would part her curtains and look at you. Eye contact would be made. The curtains would close. In fifteen minutes she would be reasonably content to see you. *Welcome, welcome. Bon bini.*

There was a farmer who claimed that rays from the TWR

transmitter made men sterile. (Then his wife had a baby.) A second farmer accused TWR of making his goats sterile, but he couldn't convince anyone, either. Which is not to say the desire to distrust TWR—and have good reason—wasn't strong.

Need your moped fixed? *No problem.* Can you have it fixed by Tuesday? *No problem.* Can I pick it up Tuesday afternoon? *No problem.* Shamble up to the garage late Tuesday and find your exhaust pipe being nosed around the dirt floor by a dog. This, too, is *no problem.*

My father tried to see *no problem* not as indicative of Caribbean-style laziness or apathy—as some TWR colleagues suggested—but as a reminder that many of our attempts at controlling our environment were futile. Outcomes came, by definition. One couldn't always beckon them through sheer application of will. Boats sink, so try to enjoy anything short of fatal shipwrecks. Each TWR family, in addition to monthly checks, had an equipment fund set aside for them to cover expenses like car repair or broken appliances. If you want to support the missions in this way, my father wrote to supporters who asked, write "Hustad Equipment Fund #39-41" on your check memo and send it to TWR headquarters, and we will be grateful.

One March we began having *no problems* with the water supply. Water, when it came out of the faucet, was as brown as iced tea. This was normal. (Rust. Fill a jug and let it sit in the fridge. Once the rust particles have settled to the bottom in a thick, sludgy sediment, the water on top should be fine to drink. This takes a few hours.) But the locals were now saying that the island's water tanks were contaminated. A handful of people had been airlifted to the Curaçao hospital with liver problems. Many more complained of headaches and stiffness in the back and in the legs. When my mother went to the grocery store to stock up on canned juice, she winced at the $2.80 per can price tag. One, it was a lot of money, and for something we wouldn't even want were clean water available. Two, she didn't look forward to the look the cashier was sure to give her—the narrow look that said, *Why, aren't you spoiled, to solve your problems so easily.*

Sermons at the TWR church building drifted toward the epistles of Saint Paul during times like this. 2 Timothy 3:12 read: *Yea, and all that will live godly in Christ Jesus shall suffer persecution.*

This verse had been interpreted a few different ways. There were impersonal trials that resulted from choosing to witness for Christ, like scorpions in showers and sweaty sandals and contaminated water. These were trials due to things—sheer circumstance—the result of having decided not to pursue comfort or security. There were always going to be people who doubted your good intentions. Billy Graham had a lot to say about this: We live in a topsy-turvy world. To an upside-down man, a righteous man is an oddity and an abnormality. A Christian's goodness is a rebuke to his wickedness; his being right side up is a reflection upon the worldling's inverted position. So the conflict is a natural one. Persecution is inevitable.*

However, Christians had to be careful, Graham cautioned, not to reason backward from persecution or unpopularity. He had known professed Christians dominated by bad dispositions, snap judgments, and poor manners who nonetheless thought that people were opposed to them because of their "righteousness." It was not their goodness that people resented—it was their lack of it. We must be careful not to behave offensively, preach offensively, and dress offensively, Graham wrote, and when people shun us, blame it on the "offense of the cross." Shabby Christians were poor advertisements for Christianity, he concluded.

---

*Billy Graham, *The Secret of Happiness: Jesus' Teaching on Happiness as Expressed in the Beatitudes* (Garden City, N.Y.: Doubleday, 1955).

But overall it was to our advantage to endure misfortunes and adversities because it brought to the surface our powers of invention, our ability to name—as God gave to Adam in the Garden of Eden, and thus to all humans—and thus allowed us to shine.

✦

Our move to a blindingly white house on an isolated road that dead-ended on a hill was prompted by staff increases. TWR owned a few dozen missionary homes but needed more, and this modern white house facing nothing but scrub brush and rocks had sat empty for months. No phone line ran up this hill and there wouldn't be one for the two years we lived there.

Separating the orange-tiled front porch from our living room was a sliding glass door. In the front yard, burned-umber dirt on which nothing grew. In the backyard, volcanic rock and the occasional rat. We were offered this house because my parents could be trusted to invite people over and share the view.

Opposite our porch the hill sloped down toward Kralendijk and the coastline. Beyond that, a water so blue it taunted you not to believe it. At sunset on cloudless days we waited for the green flash that appeared the split second the sun submerged completely behind the watery horizon line. Visitors who did not believe in the green flash were handed binoculars, which really wouldn't help them see it but lent an aura of seriousness as we waited and watched the sun lower itself into the sea.

A letter to Marian petitioned for a guestbook and more Polaroid film. The kitchen had four cupboards and barely any room for dishes, so wicker paper plate holders were pulled into service so my mother could fill the porch with guests. In evangelical parlance, this was fellowship, not "entertaining" or dinner parties. Polaroids were taken and gluesticked into the guestbook and everyone was invited to leave a note testifying to what a wonderful time they had. Dessert was Libby's canned peaches, poured syrup and all into the bottom of a 9×13 Pyrex dish, a box of cake mix spread over that, finally one stick of butter cubed and evenly distributed for a strudel-like crust and baked at 350°. Dump cake. Its virtues were many but chief among them was that it was humble and quickly prepared.

Feeding people generated a certain leeway. With the sugar, the breeze, the night sky—a permission to be irreverent. Amy and I were encouraged to point out the geckos that appeared on the wall two feet below the ceiling within the hour after sunset every night.

Did they have names? Funny you should ask.

"That one's Lucille Becker," we'd say. The fat gecko. Lucille Becker was the organist on *Unshackled*.

"*That* one is Original Music," we'd add, redirecting guests' eyes to the smallest gecko. Original Music was what—per the announcer—Lucille Becker was playing on *Unshackled*.

"And *that's* Paul Freed." The largest gecko.

Not everyone felt that naming geckos after godly women and men was appropriate or a good example to set for your children. Ankles crossed. My father chuckled. Anyone who laughed sincerely was invited back once a week.

✦

That short, sharp intake of breath, surprise meeting stifled delight. This was the sound of true Christianity, I began to think—my parents' kind, not disapproving or anxious but silly, salted. A matter of creating space wherein people could be more true to an inner joy, which by definition and necessity was stripped down, simple, even wordless. (You couldn't point right at it, only gesture in its general direction.) Somewhere in the job description was inviting people to delight in the ridiculous, even if it meant we had to generate the ridiculousness ourselves.

It was also better to be thought ridiculous because then people generally let you do what you wanted to do. Also, missionaries could be a little too holy, my mother felt. No one should take themselves that seriously.

As a joke, when asked to pick up Sonia Harris, short-term worker, from the airport, she demonstrated the kind of looseness she had in mind. Sonia emerged blinking from customs and my mother introduced herself as Karen, mission hostess, delighted to welcome Sonia to Bonaire. They chatted while Sonia's suitcase cleared customs: How was the flight, did she get any sleep, wasn't the Miami airport a zoo?

It was dark by the time my mother put Sonia's suitcase into the trunk. They drove past the rows of missionary houses south of Flamingo International and onto a stretch of road lined with pitch darkness on either side. Sonia was asked: Had she been briefed on the living conditions? Did she know to expect fairly primitive accommodations? Wonderful. After a few tense minutes the car's headlights caught the glimmer of hurricane lamp light reflecting off the rearview mirrors of some cars parked at Far Beach. They pulled up slowly and cut the engine. The Olsens turned and smiled. They had strung a clothesline from their car antenna to the thatched roof of a small stone hut, doorless and painted yellow—one of fourteen such huts arranged in two neat rows parallel to the coastline. Battery-operated radios dotted the sand. Outside another hut the Waddells sat gathered around a card table eating macaroni salad off paper plates. More families beyond, moms crocheting in beach chairs, a boy with a fresh haircut and too-short shorts trying to throw and fetch at the same time, a dozen eager faces looking up expectantly at the new arrival.

My mother lifted Sonia's suitcase from the trunk—"No, no. I've got it"—and pointed at the last hut in the row closest to the water. "We're headed to that little one on the end there."

"I think you're really going to like it here," my mother said. "The weather is so beautiful. Did you bring snorkeling gear? The snorkeling is really terrific."

Sue Fisher sprang up from the folding beach chair where she had been crocheting by the light of a flashlight. "Hi, hi. Welcome," she beamed, losing her footing in the sand but recovering quickly. She was wearing a floor-length terry cloth nightgown and a sun visor. "We're so thrilled to have you here," she drawled. "And that you had a safe flight."

The entrances to the huts extended only four feet up from the sand. The interior of the huts—"Duck"—a mere six by eight feet. Sonia was now quite pale. The joke ended when my mother confessed that we lived in real houses, not doorless eighteenth-century slave huts that an adult couldn't stand up or sleep straight in. And yes, African slaves working the salt mines had actually stayed in them, grown men, how atrocious, yes, but obviously pretty sturdily built, because . . . well, here they were. *Anyhow. Let's get back in the car.*

Her unspoken message: Should you ever feel unequal to this task, look to me.

✦

Amy tried to give me Dutch grammar lessons the summer before first grade but gave up when I couldn't sit still. I was lucky, she said. The rumor that white kids didn't shower had been squashed, pretty much.

First day of school, standing outside under the shaded portico before the bell rang, I opened my mouth but nothing came out. A girl with scraped-back pigtails and firing eyes broke from the pack of staring kids and planted herself in front of me. *Waar is jouw tong?* I opened my mouth to show her. I stuck my tongue out but not so far that it could be interpreted as sticking-out-of-tongue sticking out my tongue. She nodded.

The next morning questions came like BB gun shots. Gleeful, fast. I did not understand what was being asked of me and so I stood, back to a porch column, and looked out into the bright empty playground, because if my eyes stung from sunlight I wouldn't look close to tears. At the end of the first week, the first grade *juffrouw* pulled me aside as we shuffled inside at the sound of the bell. She smiled and announced that she would only speak English to me until the end of the month.

Her translation services would stop at that time, and I'd no longer be at risk of becoming some mute teacher's pet. But I'd best figure Dutch out fast.

For reading practice we sat at our desks, arms folded and heads bent over our grammar books, and took turns reading passages out loud. I prayed that she would forget to call on me or otherwise use her authority to encourage my classmates to forget I existed. She did neither.

May-gun, your turn. Agonizingly slowly, rife with mispronunciations, my halting pauses longer than any other kid's pauses save the not-smart boy who was always talking back and getting smacked with a wooden ruler across his palms.

Louder, please. *Ik kan je niet horen, May-gun.* Louder, please.

Titters of boys and girls across the room. (I remember the walls as dark green, but that seems unlikely.) The day getting hotter. Our grammar books were custom-made for former Dutch colonial holdings. The characters in *Zonnig Nederlands* had nonwhite skin and Spanish-tinted names and their stories concerned the importance of punctuality and diligence, and how Carlos should take care not to be seen in public with torn pants. One story was about an armed burglary foiled by a dog who bites the burglar in the leg and rips his pants—a second warning against torn clothing for those who missed the first. Vocabulary lessons included the Dutch words for "dry soil" and how to assess the size of a goat relative to a circus bear. Another story featured young Rosa, who did not get up at 6:30 a.m., took long showers, kept losing her hair ribbon, and sometimes rode the bus to school instead of walking. This bus riding was only undertaken because Rosa was late, and it strained her family's finances. Worse, Rosa probably wouldn't advance to the second grade. Why? She was lazy. In fact, Rosa was an *echte sukkel*. A genuine twerp.

At recess kids switched to Papiamento and I worried about what to do with my hands as I stood at the edges of the playground, counting the minutes until it was over.

Soon a boy glimpsed an opportunity in my muteness. He took hold of my hair. When I didn't flinch, he rested his forearm on my shoulder. He ran his fingers through my hair, rubbing its blond straightness between thumb and index finger, twirling it around. The next day he again stood next to me, sucking the thumb of his right hand and entangling the left hand's fingers in the hair that grazed my shoulders. So we stood under the tamarind tree, me staring into the dirt, neither of us speaking. When the end-of-day bell rang I hurried through the gates to where my mother waited, but not so fast, I hoped, that I appeared afraid.

Are you okay? she asked. *There's an iguana in the bathroom*, I said, which was true, and which Amy, though grades ahead and occupying a different part of the school and different playground, could verify. An adult iguana had the run of the outhouse-style toilets. There was seldom any toilet paper but this wasn't news.

We did talk about the boy and his idea to use my hair as his binky. The iguana was a harder problem to solve. I decided to not go to the bathroom. To hold it all day.

But on occasion, after rushing through the school gate and scrambling into the front seat of the car, relief came early. My mother shushed soothing words about how the upholstery was luckily plastic, and we drove home, my sundress and underwear wet with urine, tears sliding down my face. She began tucking a spare pair of my underwear into the glove compartment.

She told stories—of that time—how old was she? five?— she dressed herself for Sunday school but forget to put on underwear, and—apropos of pain more generally—the story of Fat Sharon, a classmate of aunt Laura's whom nobody liked and so Fat Sharon's mom started paying Laura 50¢ for every afternoon spent playing dolls with her, that is until Marian found out and ended this cash-for-friendship scheme.

Several weeks into school I wrote my mother a note and left it on the dining room table:

Dear Mommy,

I know how you feel when I cry at school.

It's because when you say Be friendly it just reminds me of home.

And then I get lonesome.

And then I cry from lonesomeness.

By second grade my Dutch was as good as my classmates' but I'd turned into a snitch. I ran inside to the teacher after every recess teasing. Nobody likes a tattletale, *juffrouw* told me. This sounded accurate. I wondered whether I should start saying the Hail Marys instead of only mouthing along. But then God might grow more disappointed in me than He already was.

✦

She wanted to be more than Mom and mission hostess, so when a job opened up in tape traffic, my mother applied.* Tape traffic was the air-conditioned room in TWR's studio building where all reel-to-reel programs waiting to be aired were stored, ditto programs already aired that were awaiting shipment back to the States.

Tape traffic was also where portions of programs deemed unacceptable to an international audience were spliced. The process was simple: Preview the tape at double speed until

---

*This is how I imagine that meeting went: She straightens her skirt before speaking to Don, the field director. She announces she's up for the job. It was essentially administrative, wasn't it? *Filing and keeping things organized?* She'd done that, she said. At a John Deere dealership early in her marriage, then at JCPenney. Well, yes, Don says, but it also entailed screening the programs and cutting out the parts where the host said please send money to such-and-such address in Grand Rapids, Michigan. My mother nods and makes some joke about it—of course—being inappropriate to ask listeners in Caracas to send checks to Michigan. Maybe, she thought, if she seemed slightly unaware in addition to eager, her request would sound less threatening. Then comes a question she prepared for: "What about the kids?" The implication being that her working might compromise us. "What about them?" she asks, lifting her eyebrows as high they went and smiling in the ways of moms anticipating exorbitant praise for their cute, well-behaved kids. Maybe if her face said, Yes, they are adorable, aren't they, he would let her have the job.

pattern recognition clued you in that money was about to be solicited, or that U.S. politics was being discussed, then slow the tape to normal speed. Locate the beginning of the offending sentences and take out your china marker, place a white line on the tape. Locate the end of the discussion and mark that, too. Take an X-Acto knife and cut out the inappropriate portion. Cut at an angle so any sound disruption is spread out over milliseconds and undetectable. Patch the spliced ends together with a special tape.

My mother derived considerable pleasure from the fact that she did this in half the hours it took her predecessor. He'd treated it like a full-time job, and he was there, on the island, with his wife and two kids. That was crazy, she decided. So I was put in charge of locating the fundraising requests that came toward the end of *The Children's Bible Hour with Uncle Charlie*. This meant a few hours of air conditioning, always a treat and a useful hedge against impetigo, a fun after-school activity, and giggles over how high tape speeds made Uncle Charlie sound like Porky the Pig.

✦

One portion of TWR's funding came from large donors. Another came from fees paid by program producers wanting airtime on TWR. The money to pay missionary salaries was raised by missionary families themselves. Every two years suitcases were packed and every surface of the house wiped clean in preparation for our absence. "Furlough," we called these next two months, sometimes longer. We returned to the States and bunked with relatives, in guest rooms and on foldout couches, using borrowed towels, saying please and thank you. My father drank coffee after dinner, stayed up late, and practiced our slide presentation.

We always brought our own Kodak Carousel projector. Church basements were ideal locations for fundraising appeals because they typically contained banquet-hall-style rooms with adjoining kitchens. Coffee and refreshments could be served after the slide show. Small casement windows near the ceiling were easily darkened. In the quiet minutes before these presentations my father practiced bits and snippets of his talk. He paced. He muttered. Stan—in these settings he was always "Stan"—narrated, "Karen" tended to the before-and-after chit-chat, and Amy and I—"the girls"—did most of the shifting weight from one foot to the other and being bashful. Our staging area was usually the room where brides dress for their weddings. We examined ourselves in full-length bathroom mirrors, straightened our skirts with restless, sweaty hands, and made sure our hair wasn't too wrong. That the dress or skirt was a hand-me-down, and in all probability donated to the missionary clothing barrel by a member of the audience, dialed up the sense of responsibility.

People started trickling in a full half-hour before the show. Some had pledged $20 a month. A great-aunt in Iowa whose second husband had left her the small fortune he'd earned in the manufacturing of hog watering equipment—she gave us $150 a month. Old people predominated. Some were frail and required walkers. Some felt guilty for living lives that were indistinguishable from the average American's. They gave to foreign missionaries, felt a little less ordinary and so forgiven. When the pastor got up to thank everyone for coming, he thanked them for having come out on a Sunday evening when so many football games and made-for-television miniseries competed for their attention. Everyone bowed heads as the pastor thanked God for sending us His Son. Then it was my father's turn.

"I'm just going to tell you a little bit about what we do on Bonaire, and what life is like on Bonaire," he'd start. He didn't want to convey that poor people were more spiritually pure, because that's something wealthy people said on vacation as they sat and ate breakfast on their verandas. *Look*, they'd say, *that toothless old brown lady who just emerged from a shack with a basket of plantains on her head, look how content she is.* And yet he did want to communicate that it was okay to be deprived, somehow. Then the slides: The red obelisk on Far Beach. ("Bonaire is so flat and barren that from a distance even an experienced sailor could mistake it for open sea.") The beach at Hotel Bonaire. ("You can see why people come here on vacation.") A red rag draped over a goat skull and nailed to a tree. ("What you're looking at here is a fence surrounding a *kunuku*, or farmhouse, and what they've done is place this skull on the fence as a Keep Out sign for evil spirits.") The rusting ruins of an unfinished resort abandoned by developers who had run out of money. (Spoke for itself.) Missionary kids using the ruins as a playground, only mildly inconvenienced by the garbage and broken beer bottles and ashes strewn about. (Subtext: Christians found opportunity where others saw a void.)

Closing arguments came in the form of letters sent in by TWR listeners. From Bolivia: "I am praying to God that you will keep on the air and I feel that I will take Jesus soon as my savior." From Natagaima, Colombia: "In this town there were few believers, and through your programs many have been converted." From Curaçao: "Please write and tell me of the Lord. I wish so much to obtain eternal peace. I do not lack for anything, but I do not have peace. I know many people who have received the Lord and live very happy with their families. I also want to experience that."

The imperfect earnest English helped make my father's point that these people needed to hear of the glorious day when Jesus would come again, and the kind and patient people of this planet would be rewarded for putting up with a lot of nonsense. Progress had been made on this front, halting though it was. During Bonaire's 1969 election season, one of the candidates— Wanga, his name was, a man from Rincón—had dressed up in a Fidel Castro costume to campaign. So had some of his fans. And while TWR steered clear of politics in all its on-air commentary, that this wasn't happening anymore was a sign that people were no longer looking to government to solve their problems.

After the slide presentation, well-wishers approached us one by one in an impromptu receiving line. Each left a respectful pause between the last greeter and their own arthritic handshake. Old men in sports coats were most solicitous of all. We verified the dangers goats presented to hibiscus flowers, and that it was our job to close the gate when we went anywhere, otherwise they'd be all gone, all the flowers, upon your return, anything red, actually, even if it was, like, a dishrag, and yes it's true we checked our shoes for scorpions every morning. *Uh-huh*, I'd say, *and Bonaire is so small it doesn't even show up on the map*. I loved announcing the fact that Bonaire did not appear on most maps. I relayed this information ecstatically, as if it were wondrous and fun. I was convinced the disrespect of cartographers lent us a certain distinction. Amy and I were prompted to say something in Papiamento and complied, smiling until our cheeks ached.

Families and retired couples who were not regular supporters but who made occasional donations to Hustad Equipment Fund #39-41 invited us over for casseroles and dinner rolls and dessert. In exchange for their helping us pay for car repairs, we exuded serenity. We communicated that our serenity was the result of our life choices, not in spite of them.

Raising support entailed little to no control over the food you ate. When hostesses asked if you'd like a little bit of this or that, "Yes, please" and "Yes, thank you" were the only right answers. If you said "No, thank you," she would ask, "Are you sure?" as if you couldn't be trusted to know your appetites. But you never said "No, thank you," because Jesus wouldn't refuse anyone's casserole, so we couldn't, either.

In the car on the way to these nice people's houses, Amy would remind me of the differences between acceptable Bonaire behavior and acceptable United States behavior. "You know you

don't have to wait for ants here, Nano," she'd say upon arriv..
as we clambered out of the backseat.

"*Ja.* Pfft! I know that." Then I'd punch her in the arm
because she was distracting us from clue collection. A pathway
made of irregularly shaped flat rocks winding from sidewalk to
front door was a sign of good food. A stick-straight cement
walkway promised a less enticing meal, often casserole made
with shoestring potatoes and cream of mushroom soup, canned
string beans that left puddles of soupy green on the plate. Living
room furniture held more clues. We came to associate dark
brown couches with milk served in scratched plastic glasses.

After dinner, adults returned to the living room to discuss
the assassination attempt on Pope John Paul II and how Ronald
Reagan had upset people by nominating Sandra Day O'Connor
to the Supreme Court. (His inauguration ceremony Bible verse
had been so promising, after all—2 Chronicles 7:14: *If my people, which are called by my name, shall humble themselves, and
pray, and seek my face, and turn from their wicked ways; then
will I hear from heaven, and will forgive their sin, and will heal
their land.*)

My mother talked liltingly of pious silliness. One formerly
loyal TWR supporter, for instance, had ceased giving to the
mission upon discovering that we did not quote exclusively from
the King James Bible on air. This was code for: Some people
can be pretty particular but as Christians we can't be discouraged by quirky personalities.

If our hosts had young children, Amy and I were escorted
down closet-lined hallways into first-floor bedrooms for a show-
and-tell of brand-new board games and toys that required
Duracell batteries. No, we didn't have Operation or Atari, we'd
reply. Yes, we were familiar with Strawberry Shortcake. We
weren't, ha, totally, you know, totally out of it, Amy assured the
older kids. We had a TV on Bonaire, it had one channel. *Hart
to Hart*; *Magnum, P.I.*; *Casper the Friendly Ghost.* Our parents
let us watch it.

When toy displays spilled over into the living room, interrupting adult conversation, my father skirted the edges of politeness with enthusiastic delivery of a noncompliment.

"Wow, it's like a Showcase Showdown in here," he'd exclaim.

If there were no children in the house to drag us to their rooms and introduce their possessions, I staked out a spot on the living room carpet, insisting that I liked sitting on the floor, which was true, but it was also true that I liked sitting where it would be hard for anyone to try to talk to me. They'd have to bend over, and that was awkward, especially if they were old, so they'd give up. I wanted to be able to keep my eye on everybody, too. I kept a close eye on the hostess because it was she who, wiping hands on apron as she took a break from kitchen cleanup, would volunteer to produce things for my entertainment. She might return from rummaging in the hall closet with a stack of picture books in hand. These might be picture books about the life of Jesus, which was always a letdown, but we couldn't say *No thanks, I know this stuff already.*

Eventually Amy started bringing her own books. *The Lion, the Witch, and the Wardrobe* and *The Westing Game* and *The Witch of Blackbird Pond* and *When Hitler Stole Pink Rabbit* and Nancy Drew. (That these were not exclusively Christian books raised wary eyebrows. Supporters would look to my father's face to see if he, head of household, approved. He did.)

Opinions of the meal were saved for after dinner, after the click of seat belts buckling, the click that signaled the end of the shift. My mother made it clear, however, that childlike opinions about what was edible were absolutely of no interest to anyone. Whenever I met picky eaters I stared hard so I could get a sense of just how cold their blood ran. I didn't know that was an option, to pass on a meal prepared for you.

✦

Returns to the island were eased by PTLs. They glutted my mother's letters. *Praise the Lord!* that when Berni Lusse came to pick us up at the airport, and her foot went completely through the floorboard of our car that we'd left parked at the transmitter site, nothing worse happened. *PTL!* for rusted-out motor vehicles, for the fact that unlike missionaries in Argentina, we didn't have to contend with prices going up 400 percent. *PTL!* for mousetraps that worked so we felt less beset by wildlife upon return to our relatively primitive un-air-conditioned, insect-heavy existence. Weeks after fundraising furloughs were also marked by an abundance of loot. Chris Nelson, skeptical husband of one of our Minneapolis supporters and Northwest Airlines employee, would be thinking of us. Chris worked in lost luggage and had jurisdiction over never-claimed suitcases. When the mood hit he would take one home, empty it of its contents, and after a trip to the grocery store, refill it. The suitcase would be put back on a plane with a tag with our name on it. Inside: Gallons of milk, frozen. Boxes of Double Stuf Oreos. Jell-O. Kool-Aid. Crayons. Band-Aids. Bedsheets imprinted with heat-transferred 8.5 × 11 crayon drawings made by Trinity Lutheran Church Sunday school classes, with Amy's and my names mingling with drawings of Noah's ark and rainbows and bearded men in sandals—Jesus's disciples, like us, happy for these handouts.

✦

LATER I ask my dad whether missionaries played office politics.

"I got in trouble with some of my coworkers."

"Oh yeah?"

"Well, when I started working more in programming, at the studio, I butted up against the people who didn't want to play Caribbean music. Anything with a beat, syncopation, you know, the kind of stuff you actually hear on Caribbean streets, the steel drums—they didn't want that. They wanted to play the same dusty hymns you'd hear at a church service of old Lutherans in Fargo. But music with 'too strong a beat' was . . . forbidden."

"Right."

"Nothing you could dance to. Make you want to move your hips, too."

"God forbid!"

"Oh no. Too strong a beat was bad."

"So TWR basically appointed itself dance chaperone for all of South and Central America. Ruler in hand, pelvises at least twelve inches apart, etcetera."

"And every day, we'd get requests for 'One Day at a Time.' People just loved that record. Loved it."

"I remember."

"Drove me nuts."

"TWR had the old Tennessee Ernie Ford version. That *durnnnn . . .*"

Tennessee Ernie Ford was best known for his recording of the coal mining dirge "Sixteen Tons." *Sixteen tons and what do you get? Another day older and deeper in debt.* More clearly I recalled the chilled air in the studio—one of the few places on the island that was air-conditioned—and the tall stacks of LPs on plywood shelves that stretched from carpet-tiled blue floor to soundproof-paneled ceiling.

"How that ever got approval to be played, I've no idea— Bit of a mystery to me still. Theological wasps' nest, basically."

"What didn't you like about it?"

"Well I just thought it was questionable. You know, historically speaking. 'One day at a time' is a fine message, but in the second verse where it says that everything is worse now than it was then. That just didn't, doesn't, strike me as correct or a particularly biblical way of looking at things. And then . . . you know . . . for many people . . . what? 1981? worse than the Plague, the Holocaust, worse than slavery?"

"Good point."

"But people loved it. We'd get so many letters asking us to play it. Every day. I mean—"

"It was popular."

"Hugely. We cued it up all the time. I mean, eventually I just accepted it. Realized that for a lot of people in the Caribbean, or in South America, it was a good message. Because for a lot of our listeners . . . life was crappy. So *stairways to climb, give me the strength to get by*, one day at a time, was meaningful to them."

"Uh-huh."

"Because that's what poverty is, really. Or for people living in poverty, though that's such a strange expression, like poverty is a part of town. Just this relentless sameness . . . Variety costs money."

"At least enjoyable variety, not oh-goodness-here-comes-a-different-person-to-rob-and-exploit-me kind of variety."

"I did play some other stuff, stuff that I thought would go over well, but people complained."

"What? Who?"

"Oh, you know . . . the stricter Southern Baptists."

"How did they—"

"Mostly it was anonymous. People dropped notes in the interoffice mail complaining about some of the song selections. Saying well maybe we ought to review the process by which songs received official approval to be played on the air."

"Whatever is good, whatever is pure—"*

"Exactly."

"Anonymous notes."

"Yep."

"But there are plenty of verses in the Bible that speak of dancing, right? Hands in the air, clap your hands, dance type of—"

"Yeah. 'Course. Plenty."

"_____." I tried an interview technique he had taught me:

---

*The same verse, Philippians 4:8, would be prized by junior high youth group counselors: *Finally, brothers and sisters, whatever is true, whatever is right, whatever is pure, whatever is lovely, whatever is admirable—if anything is excellent or praiseworthy—think about such things.*

just don't talk when it's your turn to talk and the interviewee will keep going.

"But what you have to understand is a lot of these missionaries just wanted to export what worked—so to speak—in Grand Rapids, Michigan, and what they had grown up with, and plunk it down in other parts of the world. The Panama Canal was another big debate."

"The Panama Canal."

"Some of the programs from the States had all this commentary about how Carter should never have signed that treaty, how God wanted the U.S. to retain ownership or control or whatever. And I didn't really think that was a good way to win people over in Central America."

"Probably not."

"No. Then there were the hurricane maps."

"The what?"

"When I was hosting *Caribbean Morning Sounds* with Bob Ketchersid, we had these hurricane tracking maps that we offered free to anyone who wrote in to request one. They were printed in the States, and on the perimeter were color photos from travel brochures and stuff and they looked real nice."

"Something to put on the wall."

"Clear black lines with longitude, latitude, and so on, so you could figure out how long you had before you had to board up the windows. And it should have been a simple thing, a nice gesture—but no."

"How so?"

"Well, some people insisted on stuffing the envelope with the map full of gospel tracts. Because they gotta save 'em! They'd put the map in and include gospel tracts also. And I said, well—I made quite an issue of it, and it was a big blowup. But I felt, no, unless someone asks for tracts, we shouldn't send them. We should send them what they asked for."

"Right."

"Now, fine. If you wanted to enclose a letter saying, *If you'd like to know more about Jesus*, or whatever the case may be, *Let us know and we'll send you some more stuff.* But no, they were just insistent that we stuff 'em in there whether listeners wanted them or not! We can't waste this opportunity! And I as program director said no, I'm not going to, I don't want to . . . be part of some bait and switch, essentially."

"Right."

"And as you say, for a lot of people it, the map, it was just something free to put on the door, you know. People loved them. We sent them out by the boatload."

"_____."

"It's just . . . first things first, if you want to reach people, you give them what they ask for. No more. Not yet."

Eventually I realized my mother had been busy doing the same, or similar. When missionary kids came over to our house to play she insisted no one call her Mrs. Hustad. *Call me Karen. Mrs. Hustad is my mother-in-law*, she'd say. But these missionary kids had been trained to understand that calling adults by their first names was disrespectful. So they persisted, and a tug-of-war ensued.

"Mrs. Hustad."

Karen.

"Mrs. Hustad."

Karen.

She persisted in correcting them until they felt her full meaning: Call people what they ask to be called.

✦

A knock on the door, and because I was nearest I opened it. My father just stood there, water running down his face and shirt, his mouth hanging open to catch flies. He never breathed through his mouth like that. We never breathed through our mouths like that.

"I wiped out," he said. "Walked the rest of the way."

He had hurt his arm and his leg but didn't think any ribs had been broken. His scooter was fine. No puddle jumper to the Curaçao hospital was required, but he was badly shaken. When Amy emerged from her bedroom—all she had been able to do since a short trip to Ecuador was sleep and throw up and reread old Nancy Drew mysteries—she confirmed that Stan looked positively terrible.

Dr. Welvaart put his arm in a simple sling. He had just lost some skin; nothing was broken. My father did not derive any satisfaction from physical pain, not in the way some men seemed to.* He took it as a personal affront and went to bed early.

That night during tuck-in I confessed to my mother that the accident was all my fault.

"I prayed for the rain," I said. "Two days ago. I was tired of the heat and I wanted it to rain and so I prayed that it would rain."

"Oh honey." My mother stopped tracing the Sunday school drawings on my sheets with her index finger. She took off her glasses. "It wasn't your fault."

To me it seemed an open-and-shut cause-and-effect case. Prayer mattered, God listened to our prayers, I had prayed for something to happen, that something had happened, ergo, etc.

My mother kept on shaking her head. "That's not—that's not how it works, sweetheart." She smiled her sleepy smile, the one where her cheeks barely budged but her eyes crinkled.

She asked what record I wanted to go to sleep to. "Debby Boone," I said. She placed her hands on her knees and stood up, hit the light, leaving the door open a crack so by the time

---

*Like the shirtless fishermen down at Lac Bai, proud of their scarred forearms and showily careless when handling machetes. Or the TWR men who worked the transmitter towers. They let their skin burn and tan and burn again until their skin could not get any darker, the whites of their hazel eyes appearing perpetually red-rimmed.

Debby was singing about how if she ever thought she could make it on her own, *to please pull her back, God*, I was asleep.

✦

TWR executive Jack Hicks proposed a change of scenery in January 1983. That conversation inspired this paragraph in the next Hustad prayer letter to supporters:

> Our Mission has asked us to think of new responsibilities, possibly in other parts of our world. We solicit your prayers on behalf of our decisions and what might follow. We want to rest in the knowledge that when we belong to the Lord, we are "sojourners" in this world and should not "pound the tent pegs down too deeply."

Hicks informed my parents that TWR was working on a brand-new, very exciting project. Possibly in Holland, he said. No more Netherlands Antilles but the actual Netherlands. Or, Hicks continued, TWR may expand facilities in Monte Carlo. It remained to be seen. "We could really use your hostessing skills," he said to my mother. "And your teaching ability," to my father.

I heard of the relocation plans one night as my mother tucked me in, Debby Boone again in the background. She played with my hair, combing her fingers through strands splayed against the pillowcase, still fresh and not sweaty from sleep. *We're going to be moving to a foreign country*, she said.

"I don't want to live in a foreign country," I said.

"That's too bad," she said. "Because you live in one now."

We started packing for somewhere, Europe, within the month. (My mother to Marian and Orville: ". . . at least our leaving has been announced now so we can openly talk about it. We just don't know where or when exactly! I'm anxious to know if it will be Monte Carlo or Holland or ? but it really doesn't matter too much I guess . . .")

Pastor Hoke—who had replaced Pastor Bock and Pastor Ashton after him—was a favorite of my father's. His last sermon to TWR Bonaire staff before returning to retired life in Pennsylvania coincided with our last weeks on the island. He was concerned, he said, over small changes he had witnessed over the past year. People were accumulating unnecessary things and attitudes. He urged young families who had not been on the island long not to try to transform Bonaire into a facsimile of their stateside existence. They had left America, he reminded them, and this leaving couldn't just be literal. If they were to be effective ministers of the Gospel of Jesus, it would not do for them to be seen as U.S. ambassadors. It would not do for them to import too much of the American way of life, or fill their homes with large televisions and VCRs.

In his sermon notes, which my father asked for and kept, Pastor Hoke made three suggestions:

1. Some of you might want to consider a change of location.
2. Learn to adjust to changing situations (ways of life).
3. Try to be as flexible as possible within the framework of convictions.

Saint Paul's letter to the Colossians provided the structure for the sermon's conclusion. Pastor Hoke promised never to cease praying for the people he had met on Bonaire, never to cease desiring that they be filled with wisdom. He would pray that they walked always in ways worthy of the Lord, do work that bore good fruit, and ever increase in knowledge of God. He wanted them to choose carefully when choosing what to love. He wanted them to be able to take anything this earth offered or leave it, for their lives were with God in Christ. Anger, wrath, malice, filthy speech—all these things had to be placed outside the gates of their homes. Plus they needed to remember there was neither Canadian nor American, Spanish nor Portuguese, German nor Swiss, Baptist nor Brethren, Lutheran nor Mennonite, but Christ was all and in all. And as the elect of God, beloved people, they were to be known for their mercies, their kindness, humility, meekness, and patience.

Leaving was in the air. Our cats had always come and gone as they pleased. They'd go for fifteen minutes, they'd go for a hundred twenty minutes. Slipped through gates and under bushes. But now both Shy Di and Mindy had been gone for over twenty-four hours.

"They'll come back," Mom assured us. "They'll come back when they're hungry."

"It's been two days." Amy's cheeks puffed with indignation. "Two days," she repeated. When Amy was upset she spoke as if she were Queen Susan of Narnia and being paid $1 for each syllable. She shot me a look that said *Maybe if you started whining, too, that would be helpful thank you very much*. Saltwater dripped down the backs of our legs onto the tile floor but our mother could not be persuaded to worry with us.

"Well, do you want to go look for them?"

We changed out of wet swimsuits and put on our school sandals and turned left at the road because someone had said, weeks ago, that he had spotted our cats at the Flamingo Beach Club once. We stuck to the side of the road that let us face oncoming traffic. I had to run-skip to keep up with Amy, who was walking as precisely and briskly as she'd been talking earlier.

Blond hair, both of us, so we could walk through the gate without being questioned. We meandered our way under the canopy of palm and bougainvillea to the seaside side of the hotel, where the pool was surrounded by lounge chairs arranged in a circle four rows deep. Women with hair pulled back tight, red lipstick, bikinis like the ladies on *Magnum, P.I.*, stretched across lounge chairs, holding their place in Sidney Sheldon paperbacks with long fingernails. Ice clinked in sweaty glasses and *chibichibi*s chirped and darted over sugar bowls. Splashes from cannonballs. A lot of strange, loud children were laughing and yelling like they owned the place, like they belonged here. In the ashtrays, cigarette butts lined with red lip prints, crumpled-up receipts.

Amy focused on a lounge chair occupant with extra-dark sunglasses and a wide-brimmed straw hat, four kids all younger than us gathered around her, all fixated on something at their bare wet feet. Amy strode up as if she knew what to say.

"Excuse me," she said, making eye contact with no one. "Hi. Nice to meet you. Those are our cats."

Mindy and Shy Di were sprawled and purring on a striped beach towel, promiscuous bellies stretched to accommodate all the little hands vying to pet them. Three open tins of Fancy Feast were shoved under the nearest lounge chair.

"Ah, of course," the woman said with a Spanish accent. "Zey could not say, ze staff 'ere, so we—"

"Sure. Okay. Thank you for looking after them." I could tell Amy didn't mean this. The cats snarled as we picked them up and clutched them towel-less to our stomachs. "Well. Okay. We have to go now. Thanks for feeding them."

The lady in the hat smiled and we hurried out of the pool area back toward the gate. Amy was walking faster now.

"Hey, wait up, Ame." Amy flung the gate open and let it slam shut behind her and did not check to see if I'd made it through.

"Heyyy." Then "Owwww," because she hadn't turned around. "My toe."

"Sorry." Amy stopped and looked at my feet to make sure there was no blood. Her eyes were glassy. Shy Di was squirming, straining against her grip.

"You're crying."

"No I'm not. Come on, let's go."

Our dog wouldn't miss us, either. A few weeks before our departure date the Fitzgeralds hosted company from Philadelphia. This family from Philadelphia had been thinking about getting a dog, Ms. Fitzgerald told our mother over the fence where the laundry lines met. They really liked our dog. Why, they, the Fitzgeralds, were leaving for furlough in two weeks, and Philadelphia was their first stop. They would be more than happy to deliver Tanya to her new home, that is, if we should determine, after praying about it, that we should give our dog to this family that wanted it.

"Sorry, Tanya," Amy and I whispered. We had been terrible dog owners, that was certain. But our parents were delighted with this dog handoff arrangement. Subtract mutt and you've one less thing to worry about when you move. God *did* attend to details, after all.

This was going to be pretty easy, we thought. Amy and I already spoke Dutch. We were all white. We would have fewer rashes. Easy.

✦

Our parents traveled ahead to Holland on reconnaissance, to find a house, install carpet at the new office, and attend Amsterdam '83, a Billy Graham conference for 10,000+ itinerant evangelists from mostly third-world countries. I was dispatched to Fairfax, Virginia, where my uncle Paul, aunt Elaine, and seven-year-old cousin Stephanie formed a strikingly blond all-American tableau in a two-story colonial on a tree-lined cul-de-sac. Every morning Paul went to work at the Pentagon and every evening Elaine gave Stephanie and me two options for dessert: three prunes or two Peanut M&M's.

Amy met me there a week later because she was nearly fourteen and had asked to stay behind in Bonaire a while longer. (You become a special guest star, she'd noticed, as soon as you announce you're leaving.) The twelfth of June was a good day for her to leave Bonaire, she explained while unpacking her suitcase with me as audience, training bras and T-shirts littering the guest room chintz. She tossed a book onto the bedspread. *The Diary of a Young Girl* by Anne Frank.

I did not follow. Amy explained that this Frank girl had also moved to Holland, like we would be doing shortly, so her diary was an appropriate book to be reading at this juncture in our lives. She, too, had been uprooted from a comfortable situation and forced to learn Dutch, etc., and anyhow, June 12 was Anne Frank's birthday, so—

In the following weeks, lessons on how to be American—to talk like Valley Girls, what to wear, gag me with a spoon, how to wrap metal barrettes with thin satin ribbons, decorate yourself, be less frumpy, enjoy these pop songs, like this boy named Mickey, because he is so fine, or like boys generally. Amy's body reacted to change by demanding ten hours of sleep each night. She went to bed early, was the last one to pad into the kitchen in the morning, and nodded off while reading.

Elaine wanted to take Amy and me shopping, but during a tense phone call with my mother it was gently suggested that we wait until we arrived in Holland so we could get a sense of what kids wore there. Amy and I were fairly agnostic on the question, but the metal barrettes wrapped with thin satin ribbons that were all the rage in Fairfax seemed less an option and more a moral requirement. There had been no pressure to look fashionable in Bonaire because everyone dressed terribly. But after a week in Fairfax, it was clear that this was a kind of naïveté best placed behind us.

Our mother wore a loose-fitting black cotton jacket when we were reunited at the Minneapolis–St. Paul airport. We pointed out that she was wearing black. *I know*, she said. She'd bought it at an outdoor flea market in Amsterdam—very exciting. She was aglow. They'd found a house. Amy and I would get our own rooms. Both our schools were within walking distance.

In Minnesota, we had to consider how much more Americanness we should absorb because there was the chance that not much of this education would be useful in Holland. We waited. One anxious afternoon in Aunt Laura's fixer-upper Victorian, I flouted instructions not to horse around on the staircase. Some balusters were loose. A swift accidental kick on the midflight landing sent a loose baluster tumbling toward my mom, who had walked through the front door seconds earlier. She was setting her purse down when—*thock*—a twenty-four-inch hardwood spindle landed a direct hit just above her left temple.

This was the first time I'd seen an adult fail to fight off tears. Normally she would reassure me that accidents happened. She didn't do that this time, and I was sure I was rotten to the core.

That night it was Amy's turn to sit on the edge of my bed. Mom and Laura had returned from the emergency room and were speaking softly downstairs over slices of French Silk pie from Poppin' Fresh Bakery and cautious sips of white wine.

"They knew the bal—that it was loose. They could have fixed it before we got here." I wiped escaped tears from my cheeks and Amy fixed a distracted stare on the corner of the chenille bedspread.

"You need to be more careful, Nano."

✦

I find a copy of the daily newspaper printed for Billy Graham's Amsterdam '83 conference. Amid the prayer requests were messages like this:

1. God measures success by the numbers. Conference organizers expressed hopes that techniques learned at the conference would enable the travelling preachers in attendance, who typically drew 200 or 300 persons a night in their small

villages or favelas or wherever they came from, to double or triple their audience.

2. God can impose His will on electrical gadgets, and it is appropriate to ask Him to do so. So please pray that conference proceedings be unhindered by technical glitches.

HOLLAND

p. 27. Everyone takes it for granted that facts and truth are one; and if God is no longer regarded as true in our day it is because he does not seem to be a fact.

p. 27, cont. To have a religion there is no need of creeds and dogmas, ceremonies and rites: all that is necessary is that men and women in the mass should adhere to it with their hearts. Now, if we try to see what people as a whole worship in our day, it is easy to perceive that whatever form their worship may take, it is always connected with the "fact." We need only look through illustrated magazines to see that this is so.

p. 28. Anyone who questions the value of the fact draws down on himself the most severe reproaches of our day: he is a "reactionary," he wants to go back to the "good old days." Those who make these reproaches do not realize that such questioning of the fact is perhaps the only revolutionary attitude possible at the present time.   —*The Presence of the Kingdom*

✦

Upon arrival in Holland: air that smelled of crisp lettuce. Occasionally briny, vaguely fishy, but whisper-thin and cool. It did not press in like Bonaire air, so heavy and presumptuous it seemed to touch you everywhere, on your ankles and neck, as if to help you stand upright under hot sun. We looked out the train window at the green, flat horizon line dotted with low-slung farms and Holstein cows. The whole country looked like Legos, like a cheese and mayo sandwich sliced into four even triangles.

The International Training Communications and Research Center—or Intracare—was housed in a spacious three-story home that had sheltered a prosperous Dutch family in the early 1900s but had long since been given over to office space. On the ground floor was a conference room with floor-to-ceiling paned glass windows. Across the hall were administrative offices, and toward the rear, the dining room and its pea green walls, and behind that an industrial kitchen. A wide central staircase led upstairs to more offices, a library, and a lounge. The third floor held a series of dormitory-style bedrooms containing a total of sixteen twin IKEA beds with white IKEA sheets and particleboard IKEA nightstands. This is where the students would sleep.

The reason for Intracare was the notion that cynics who coolly remarked that Europe was incontrovertibly post-Christian were mistaken. Dr. Freed was convinced that Europe's future would be a Christian one. TWR's small foothold in the Netherlands would encourage that trend and also train itinerant evangelists from less-developed countries in radio production, so that an evangelist from Ghana could produce his own programs instead of some missionary organization sending a guy from Grand Rapids, Michigan, to do it.

TWR had practical reasons for locating the center in Holland. Every godforsaken country offered at least one weekly direct flight to Schiphol Airport, and the Netherlands' visa restrictions were not that restrictive. You could be from Iran and have a criminal record, as Intracare student "Tony" did, and pass through immigration unruffled.

My father would teach and develop the curriculum. My mother would help run the show. Meals had to be cooked and common spaces kept clean. She would know when to buy more toilet paper, and to smile encouragingly when a man far from home tried foreign foods. She knew the exact moment a quick nod helped someone stop hesitating before taking the first bite. She would introduce students to *friet met mayonaise* and chauffeur them to tulip fields in April.

The decision to set up shop in Bussum, specifically, in a tranquil area in North Holland known as Het Gooi, an area that enjoyed a nationwide reputation as one of the best places to meet snobs, was made by Simon Osmund. Average household income in Het Gooi was high, and its children differentiated themselves from poorer Dutch kids by their distaste for soccer. Het Gooi preferred field hockey. Why Intracare here and not, as some would have expected, in one of Amsterdam's dingier suburbs was a mystery.

Simon, who stood tall and pale in gray suits, didn't feel the need to explain his choice, and the location was inarguably lovely—no one denied that. Simon was Scottish but spoke in plummy BBC World Service tones, as if a lectern was ever before him. I imagine him clearing his throat, fidgeting with his starched shirt cuffs, and explaining Intracare's mission this way:

> It serves not only TWR's own technical, programming, and administrative staff, but also the leaders and workers of other related organizations. Our purpose is simple: to help Christian leaders and workers everywhere to understand radio's enormous potential as an evangelistic and discipling tool, and to give them the knowledge and skills they need to use this tool to bring people to Christ and help them grow in Him.

Curriculum drafted at Intracare would be tested in Nairobi, Hong Kong, Delhi, São Paolo, and anywhere else radio was used to spread the word.

Intracare would also assist pastors working at the grassroots levels of radio ministry and equip them to record messages in their own tribal languages and dialects. They wanted to investigate: Could they neutralize any excessive Western influence? Western communication models tended to be monological and market-based. TWR had learned this didn't fly in Latin America and suspected it was true in other parts of the world also.

The thing is, Simon said, *is that people know deep down what that Truth is. It just needs to be brought to life.* Radio programming was a God-given means of doing this. Why? Three reasons:

1. Its personal nature. Regular listeners developed the sense that they knew a radio announcer. An intimate relationship developed despite the fact that they'd never met face-to-face.

2. Enormous multiplication of effort. Broadcast over a local station and you could address an entire city. Begin enabling small broadcasters on an international scale and you could potentially reach everyone in every country, speaking any dialect.

3. Cost effectiveness. Radio facilities required a significant capital outlay at the outset. But the price per person reached ultimately proved minimal.

When the Intracare students began arriving from far-flung parts of the world, they got out of cars with legs stiff from sixteen-hour flights. Some needed help using the shower. One tap for hot and cold water? They had not witnessed this before. Some had traveled for two days to reach Holland. Those who didn't have a coat were lent a coat for the season. A ritual began of trying on coats in the hallway, testing the tug of fabric against shoulders, the length of sleeves, to see if this coat was part of God's story.

On the first night that the full class was safely there and their meager luggage deposited next to their assigned IKEA bed and nightstand, we trundled over to the pancake house down the street past the train station. A missionary parade: men all shades of brown and all manner of accents, escorted by men and women speaking English English and American English both, assorted children, giggling, self-conscious, all in shabby coats, everyone polite, filling up that tiny pancake house with its brown walls and delft tiles surrounding an unused fireplace and light fixtures made of old wagon wheels. We held clammy hands and bowed heads before the meal, muttering thanks to God for the great things he hath done and was about to do. Silently I thanked God that we walked instead of drove because we'd just been informed by our Dutch neighbors—not Christians, they'd already told us—that the Mitsubishi station wagon my parents had purchased that summer was too large a car. Not surprising, they continued, that an American family would have selected such a big car, but yes, definitely a choice we had made and a slightly disappointing one.

✦

"What was your first meeting with Simon Osmund like?" I ask my father.

"That memory is foggy, lost, or deliberately forgotten."

✦

Our first Sunday in Holland we drove to Amsterdam for church and realized that Dutch highways were smaller than American ones and favored Renaults, so our neighbors had been right. My mother pointed out the graffiti covering the dilapidated buildings on the city's outskirts. OOPS, WRONG PLANET in drippy white capitals was her favorite. Why English, we wanted to know. TV, was the answer. A lot of American TV programs aired here.

The closer we got to the city center, the browner and older the buildings became. We gingerly navigated through narrow streets and parked the enormous Mitsubishi alongside a canal called Groenburgwal—"Grune-berg-wall"—near which, my mother promised, we'd find our new church. She warned us about dog poop on the sidewalks. *No pooper-scooper laws here*, she added. The air was chilled and threatening to rain. It would feel like this most of the time.

She explained "Church of England" to us: proper hymns and liturgy and a sanctuary full of British expats.

"Weirdos," Amy volunteered.

"I wouldn't say 'weird.'"

They settled on "eccentric" and explained to me what that meant. In our family mind, expats and missionaries occupied different categories. We did not call ourselves expats. Expats had secular agendas. My mother also explained that a Rembrandt painting had hung in Christ Church before it was a church. That picture of guys in black hats and lace collars sitting around a table that you see on the Dutch Masters cigar box? That one. She was using the same *This is pretty impressive* voice she'd used for Bonaire visitors who'd never seen real driftwood before.

Amy had questions. "What was it before it was a church?" If a detail was ever left out, Amy scowled until the situation was rectified.

"It was a drapery guild."

"Drapery gill?"

"Guild."

"Gild."

"Like a club for fabric makers. Watch out for the bikes."

She slammed her arm against my chest to prevent me from stepping into the path of an oncoming cyclist. She waved her arm to signify all of the houses lining the canal. Built in the seventeenth and eighteenth centuries.

Directly inside the church building's entrance was a marble-floored cubbyhole foyer with mysterious doors leading to mysterious spaces. Through another heavy wooden door was an open-air passageway with vines growing up the walls on either side, bikes propped up the entire length. Thirty small steps later another wooden door and another dark foyer with chiseled inscriptions and then a sliding door and suddenly a smiling old man was handing us red hymnals. At the end of each pew were two-hundred-year-old doors with sticky handles. Wooden seats were covered by worn red velvet seat cushions, and at the top of the pew's wooden back, where an adult's shoulder blades hit, a half-inch ledge "so you don't fall asleep."

Above the altar hung a carving of a golden lion and a white unicorn holding a shield between them. *We are going to church in Narnia,* Amy said. *Mr. Tumnus is going to come running down the aisle any minute.*

Afterward, our mother walks us past dog poop and broken car windows and explains that car stereos were often stolen and sold for money to buy heroin—"an illegal drug"—and would we like to see the red-light district after lunch?

We did.

It was my turn to sit in the front seat as she navigated the district's tight corners with the enormous Mitsubishi. She put her tour guide voice back on.

"When you see a red light by the door or in the window, that's one. Or sometimes they just have a red curtain to show that they're in business."

We saw our first prostitute balanced on a stool behind a large picture window. The red curtains were a dusty velvet just like the pew cushions at Christ Church only pushed to the sides and beckoning, in contrast to the locked pew doors. The lady was wearing pale blue briefs with loose elastic, and nothing else. Wispy blond hair hung down to her shoulders, her ample breasts drooping over a white belly suggestive of french fries and milk swigged straight from the carton. She looked bored. Her glance flitted about, never focusing for long on any particular thing.

The car behind us honked.

"What?"

"When the curtain's drawn, that means they have a customer."

Prostitution looked like something you'd do between cleaning toilets and folding laundry. As if the lady in the blue underwear wasn't wearing pants because she was doing a load of darks.

How much familiarity with the preoccupations of the secular world was safe? At what point would sophistication turn into something that interfered with your ability to see God? This we all wanted to know, each in our own lips-shut, backseat-of-the-car way.

Mostly I was confused. The women standing in the picture windows were not what I considered beauties. My eight-year-old logic was as follows: Anyone misbehaving was taking a mortal risk, and so must possess something that made mortal risk easier to brave. A quality like good looks, possessions like royalty or cigarettes.

✦

Amy's first day of high school in Holland was complicated by the downing of Korean Airlines flight 007 by two Soviet air-to-air missiles. The story had been all over the news. Two hundred sixty-nine people headed from Anchorage to Seoul were killed. The Soviet Politburo insisted that the Korean pilots were flying over Soviet airspace after having failed to identify themselves and that the Korean planes had proceeded toward the Sea of Japan in defiance of direct orders and so at the very least should have expected to be shot out of the sky. The U.S. secretary of state was calling it a brazen breach of international protocol; the Russians were saying *Don't be crazy, we don't know what you're talking about*; and President Ronald Reagan upped the ante by calling it an act of barbarism that only a society with a wanton disregard for human life would engage in.

The kids at Godelinde Gemeente high school wanted to know if Amy, as an American, had any feelings on the matter. *Was this a deliberate provocation on behalf of the Soviets*, her classmates wondered. *Or was Reagan just using this incident to push forward his proposal for more dollars for more and more nuclear weapons for America's already fearsome military arsenal?*

"It sounds kinda like the beginning of World War One all over again," Amy answered. It was all horrible and awful, she added.

The Dutch kids had a lot of questions for us about the United States, most of it based on the limited bits of media and advertising exported to their country. *Did American houses look like the houses on* Dallas? *Did our family own horses? Were we truly allowed to drink Coca-Cola in the mornings? Did we eat at McDonald's a lot? Reagan seemed stupid, yes?** Where in the *Yunited States* was Amy from?

---

*In April 1982, the Netherlands' Queen Beatrix is greeted at the White House in the usual fashion—South Lawn photo op, U.S. Army Herald Trumpets, Fife and Drum Corps, and a twenty-one-gun salute. At the White House state dinner the next night: Reagan toasted the Netherlands' speed in recognizing the Continental Congress at the end of the American Revolution. How the Dutch helped shape the American landscape and character. "When thinking of this, images come to mind of Henry Hudson, in 1609, sailing up the river that now bears his name, of pilgrims embarking at Delfshaven bound for America after living twelve years in Holland, of the Dutch West India Company buying Manhattan Island and laying the foundation for a magnificent city of commerce, and of sturdy Dutch pioneers breaking ground for new farms in our Midwest." (Pause.) "I thought that I would surprise Her Majesty by telling her that each year there's a tulip festival in Holland, Michigan. She's already booked to go there." (Laughter.)

But Queen Beatrix wanted to talk about recent events that had tested the U.S.–Dutch friendship. Four Dutch journalists had been killed in El Salvador earlier in the year, and the insinuation that the United States was "somehow to blame," as one unnamed official put it, had inspired demonstrators to storm the U.S. consulate in Amsterdam, after which the Americans protested that the Dutch had failed to offer their people in El Salvador sufficient police protection. She also pointed out that Holland's recognition of the

"Minneapolis" proved to be a good answer. *Prince is from Minneapolis*, a boy with gel in his bangs and an upturned polo collar remarked. *Was she aware of this fact?* Amy nodded but confessed that she had never met Prince—*niet persoonlijk, natuurlijk. Not personally, of course.*

"Everybody's got a bomb," the boy with gelled bangs began in a raspy falsetto. "We could all die any daaaaaayyyyy." He squinted, eyes fixed on her lips. "The words to '1999,'" he explained.

"Yeah. I know that," Amy said, looking at her watch. Three more minutes until the bell would ring and no sign of the teacher. She began to feel she had applied too much lip gloss.

"You like that song?" the boy asked. He was tilting his entire desk and chair combo forward so that it balanced on the two front legs.

"Sure." She was figuring out that the best way to remove excess lip gloss was to scrape it off subtly with your teeth and swallow it.

"But tell me, *A-mie*, is it true that Americans don't really care whether we all"—he extended his arms left and right and brought them back together so palm hit palm—"*splat*? You

United States was not entirely without self-interest, as Dutch bankers saw an opportunity for profit.

She conceded that the Marshall Plan had been instrumental in rebuilding the Dutch economy after World War II. It succeeded, she said, "because the plan did not seek to impose a pattern of its own but respected the values cherished in Europe." The Associated Press interpreted this as Beatrix broaching the subject of the nuclear arms race in the "gentlest of diplomatic language." To her audience at home, it was an unambiguous suggestion that Reagan shut up and listen.

United Press International reported that Beatrix was overheard remarking to Charlton Heston that "anti-Americanism is growing, unfortunately" in Europe. Two days later, she told a joint session of Congress that a "balanced, controlled reduction of arms on all sides" was a top priority. On the last day of her five-day state visit, she helped Willem de Kooning celebrate his seventy-eighth birthday. He was living in East Hampton, New York, and traveled by helicopter to meet her.

The following month, the Dutch cabinet collapsed over economic policy disputes. When Reagan traveled to Europe later in 1982, he spun through France, Italy, the Vatican, the United Kingdom, and West Germany, but prudently sidestepped the Netherlands.

know, like you want to get at the Soviets and we are all here, basically, in the way?" As he was still tilting his desk forward, staying balanced required some legwork.

"Of course not! Of course we—"

It wasn't clear what facial expression should accompany a denial that your native country was officially ambivalent about the survival prospects of the boy you were speaking to.

Amy stormed into the house after school bemoaning the morning's wardrobe decisions to our mother. A multicolored striped Oxford shirt over pink pants and legwarmers had been a huge mistake. Also, no more lip gloss. Instead, plain white shirts, upturned collars, black, gray, and faded denim. The new rainbow.

"Oh, and another thing," she said, turning to me. "We have to stop talking like we're black." Somehow our family had overlooked this wrinkle: To native Dutch ears, a pair of pale white girls speaking Antillean Dutch was like Marcia Brady talking like . . . Amy couldn't think of a name but we got the point. Over dinner she explained. We pronounced the *n* at the end of words that ended in *n*. No one did that in Holland. End-of-word *n*'s were silent. If you did pronounce them, you were obviously from the Antilles or just weird.

The next week Amy began to find her groove. She put on face paint and joined some kids from her class at a protest against nuclear proliferation in Bussum's town square. The United States wanted to deploy on Dutch soil forty-eight NATO cruise missiles aimed at Moscow. She agreed with her classmates that this wasn't a totally awesome idea. Our parents weren't sure about the protests, however. The white face paint was a little dramatic, and the line between protesting against the United States and supporting the Soviet Union, well, who's to say where the line lay between sympathy for Communists and impatience with God.

Meanwhile, the children of the Godelinde elementary school's third grade were similarly intrigued by the new quiet American girl who barely spoke, and when she did, sounded

Antillean. They picked me second-to-last for *slagball* games, just before they picked the untouchable Nicole, who was unforgivably chubby and desperate for a friend, so she became mine.

Kids also wanted to know if the organization my family worked for was like the Evangelische Omroep, the religious broadcaster whose designated day on the Nederland 1 TV channel was Wednesday. EO announcers spoke in soothing near whispers, as if no punks with green mohawks congregated in Amsterdam's Dam Square, as if good people never raised their voices in front of the children.

No, I said, that TV station had nothing to do with what my parents were doing. *Helemaal anders. Totally different,* I said, though even in the moment I was aware that I was talking to an audience, an audience that included myself, that didn't really appreciate the distinction I was trying to formulate. My halting sentences rang defensive even as I strained for carefree. I was learning that whenever a question essentially began with *Aren't you just like so-and-so* there was little point in responding. Your inquisitor would suck in her cheeks while waiting for you to stop talking as she continued believing what she had already decided was true: You were just like so-and-so.

✦

The first disagreement over how to be effective missionaries in Holland revolved around the Intracare kitchen. Lucinda, in a voice the sound of butterflies and eyelashes, wanted Cuisinarts. She felt Christians needed to demonstrate that they were prepared to lead, and in order to demonstrate that capacity for leadership, or just an overall ineffable excellence, it helped to dabble in symbols that the broader culture recognized as indicators of quality. If witnesses for Christ surrounded themselves with subpar, off-brand appliances, the secular world could rightly accuse Christians themselves of being subpar.

My mother thought differently, as did my father, and over dinner they discussed how:

1. Intracare was housing men who were accustomed to meals cooked on hot plates.

2. Many of them came from places where it was not safe to drink the tap water.

3. That night my mother noticed a light on in the kitchen after she thought she'd closed everything up and there was Na-keel, standing over the sink, and next to it a stack of red plastic plates identical to the ones she'd placed in the trash two hours earlier. (Karen: "Can I help you?" Nakeel: "Sorry, yes. Yes, sorry. I hadn't heard you. I hadn't heard you coming." Karen: "Oh—" Nakeel: "Where I'm from—. So. So. So this would be very precious to them, to have these plates.")

4. Two big stew pots, some knives and vegetable peelers, and an industrial-size rice cooker should be enough.

5. We didn't need Cuisinarts because we'd always gotten along fine without them. Lack of sophistication ought to be the Christian's guide for shopping, my mother felt. We had eaten Spam sandwiches for dinner on Bonaire. Why? Because Spam was cheap, and available, and kids didn't really know the difference, or the low cultural associations that Spam had. So who was Lucinda trying to impress? Who did she think was watching?

6. Her dad. Every two years Orville got a new car, because Marian's brother owned a GM dealership up in Sandstone, Minnesota. Orville always insisted that the new car look as much like the old one as possible. This became difficult during the fifties, when carmakers made every year's model immediately, recognizably different from the previous year's, but Orville tried, because he was aware we all liked to watch, nearly as much as we enjoyed judging. And in any event, a humble pastor with not-so-humble habits was contemptible.

But the main reason why no money should be spent on Cuisinarts for the Intracare kitchen, my mother believed, was that when Jesus said *Do not store up treasures here on earth*, he was not simply saying that chasing after shiny objects was a waste of your time. He was saying that displaying the best and glossiest hardened hearts. Not just your own but other people's. You made it hard for people to concentrate on the work they needed to do when you were constantly distracting them with shiny stuff.

Oh, and here was another thing: if you never looked like you needed help, people probably wouldn't help you. Imagine Mother Teresa in Nancy Reagan's wardrobe instead of that lowly cotton sari. Cuisinarts just confused the issue. Cuisinarts were not meek. Cuisinarts got in meek's way.

✦

The first time we all went to the Rijksmuseum, we had to stop at every painting for five, sometimes ten seconds before we moved on to the next one, because if a person didn't stop for an appropriate amount of time and read all labels, such a person might accidentally skip over a very famous and art-historically significant painting. That might set off high-frequency alarms that let more advanced museumgoers and museum staff know a mistake had been made, and *some people* in the gallery maybe didn't understand what they were looking at and maybe didn't deserve to be in the presence of these oil paintings in the first place.

Maybe not likely, but possible: an art appreciation error caused a blue hologram of a lightbulb to form over one's head, like a crown of stupid. This was a signal to the gift shop clerks that it was okay to snicker at your mom and visitors from the U.S.A. in their white tennis shoes and give them all incorrect change. My mother started studying up on the major Dutch artists: Rembrandt, Vermeer, Frans Hals, Gerrit Dou, Adriaen van Ostade, and Vincent van Gogh said not like *Go* but violent phlegm-balled *Cough*. Then the French impressionists and postimpressionists: Monet, Manet, Corot, Pissarro, Cézanne, Gauguin, Courbet, Matisse. She worked hard to pronounce them all correctly. When that proved impossible she had the satisfaction of at least knowing which ones she wasn't pronouncing correctly, and that was some victory in and of itself.

✦

Vacation was a road trip. We drove east to Germany, then followed the Rhine into the Black Forest, then crossed into Switzerland and Austria, skipping Cologne, Munich, Geneva, and Vienna. Stan and Karen had stopped in Salzburg during their first trip to Europe in the summer of 1973 and they remembered that second-tier cities were more to their liking.

For lodging we stayed in rented rooms. In every town where we spent the night my father parked the Mitsubishi near the train station and surveyed the motley assortment of people holding cardboard signs announcing *Zimmer frei*. They had an unused room in their house and were looking to fill it.

People hoping to stretch fixed incomes by renting out stuffy second-floor bedrooms on a night-by-night basis all wore beige, it seemed to me, as if dressing conservatively lessened the risk inherent in inviting shelterless strangers passing through town into one's home. We also sensed risk, that of being killed in our sleep, so if we spotted an older lady in a beige trench coat cinched tightly at the waist, grim resignation pulled into a frown, sensible beige shoes on her feet, my father approached her, because it seemed unlikely that old ladies would wield knives, at least not long nor well enough to kill all four of us. A brief conversation—"How much?" and "How many are you?" and "Will you be wanting breakfast?" and exaggerated hand gestures indicating vague directions and the need for us to follow her—later, and we would be trudging up creaking stairs, trying to keep our bags from scuffing the beige walls, to a tidy room containing a double bed, two twin beds, nightstands, and lamps. The bedspreads were invariably dusty rose chenille and worn thin from frequent washing. The room was always deemed *fine*.

"Fine" was one of our new favorites. How are you feeling? *Fine*. How did _____ go? *It went fine*. How do I look? *You look fine*. This last variation, we'd noticed, made my mother mad, which is how our giggles over the word started. *Fine* was never fine. But we would not be killed in our sleep, at least not all four of us, not by that old woman acting alone. She appeared arthritic so we'd live another day, plus we got to experience something richer than that experienced by the average hotel guests.

In Bavaria, visiting the extended family of a Bonaire missionary, my father was excited to be able to tell people that our next-door neighbor in Holland, Mr. Visser, had been involved in building the bridge on the river Kwai while a POW in Southeast Asia. Now he and his wife lived a genteel retirement, fresh tulips always on the table. Our hosts told us of Nazi soldiers ransacking their cupboards, hauling off heirloom furniture. Stories of horror plus survival plus historical distance were well complemented by coffee and butter cake, napkins to wipe crumbs and pampered Americanness from your mouth.

Our third cloudy morning in Salzburg we visited the *Sound of Music* gazebo. The gazebo had been relocated to accommodate a gravel parking lot large enough for fourteen tour buses, weeping willows softening the perimeter. Before leaving our room Amy glanced out the window at the drizzle and refused to wear a plastic burgundy rainslicker like the ugly one I was resigned to being seen in. By the time we arrived, it was pouring rain, and although Amy dutifully joined me in counting twelve tour buses, I could tell her heart wasn't in it.

People with cameras around their necks milled about but few actually took pictures. It wasn't entirely clear what the picture would be of. The gazebo looked like a gazebo, same lines and shape as in the movie but with none of the magic. I sat down on one of two benches not covered with stacks of laminated souvenir guidebooks and observed. People disembarking from tour buses pausing on the last step before committing to terra firma. Most paused for a second on the last step to do a 180-degree scan of their surroundings. Only then did they commit to setting foot on the ground. I wondered what they were looking for. I wondered if anyone just stayed on the bus.

Amy joined me on the bench, saying nothing as she smoothed her baggy white pants over her knees. She was talking less. She was developing an understanding: it was not okay to want a souvenir guidebook, it was not cool to ride tour buses, to wear white socks or white tennis shoes or baseball caps or Hard Rock Cafe T-shirts or to speak loudly in an American accent. She had recently decided her hair was babyish fine and lacking volume, her feet too large. I wanted a souvenir guidebook but wasn't ready to admit this. Dad had wandered off somewhere because he couldn't think deep thoughts about Nazis with all these people around, we figured.

Mom approached camera in hand and singing the first verse of "Sixteen Going on Seventeen." Amy gave her a *Take my picture and I will hate you all day* look and Mom feigned surprise that her nearly sixteen-year-old daughter would not want her photograph taken at the *Sound of Music* gazebo on a day when her wet hair hung limp. As if this was a first. She told Amy that her hair looked cute and retrained her eyes on the forlorn stacks of laminated guidebooks.

"It doesn't have quite the same feeling, does it?" she said. The shabbiness of the gazebo seemed like confirmation that movie-version Liesl was prettier than the real Liesl. When Dad reappeared we walked slowly back to the Mitsubishi consoled by the thought that we weren't as naïve as the people traveling by bus. That evening we ate at a family restaurant near the Salzburg city center—the same restaurant we ate at the night before, and the night before that. Wiener schnitzel and french fries, bright lights and waiters who didn't mind our English, and the glow in all things and each other returned. We were pretty good, and we caught on quickly. Every night would be perfect if we could keep moving, I determined, unnoticed and unbothered, never stopping for long enough to be called anything or answer to anyone beyond us four.

✦

The other Holland assignment was preparing radio scripts distilling the advice of Evelyn Christensen. Christensen was a Minnesota pastor's wife who believed that prayer was very effective but most people were doing it wrong. She also believed that prayers were always answered, which meant that even when one did not receive what one asked for, or even if things had turned out badly, there was an answer in that—of some kind. If you were paying attention.

But answered prayer had a few prerequisites. Christensen cited a verse: *The effectual, fervent prayer of a righteous person availeth much*, emphasis on *righteous person*. If you were living in sin and liking it, God would not hear your prayers. The primary sin, in Christensen's book, was not accepting the lordship of Jesus Christ; pride a close second.

The next thing Christensen hoped to communicate regarding prayer was that techniques were helpful. Ideally, one prayed in small groups, one subject at a time, one person praying primarily aloud while others prayed silently along. This resolved the problem of people not really focusing on the prayer being prayed but planning what they would say once it was their turn. She had noticed in the prayer seminars she led at her own church and eventually at churches across the United States that such distractions compromised prayer's effectiveness.

Christensen also believed that it helped to keep track of separate requests to God and specific answers given. On a ledger sheet of sorts. This was particularly important if and when members of the prayer group started losing interest. Then, one needed to thank God for those specific answers to prayer. Then watch as new life flowed into it. Above all, Christensen wanted her readers to know that God did not make mistakes. When women prayed, they did not drop words into a bottomless barrel. A woman might come before God in prayer and ask for certain things, and she might see her wishes fulfilled or she might not. But regardless of whether God granted us the specific results we requested, the outcome reflected God's answer. Whatever happened to people who sought God's direction furthered God's plan.

At the same time, Christensen recommended praying not for a specific outcome, but instead for God's perfect will to be done unto you and your family. My mother clutched this advice like a life raft, a blanket, a hedge against unintended consequences.

✦

If I had known about the content of these radio scripts—and I didn't—I might have wondered what about that message appealed. (He placed a lot of pressure on performance, this God.)

A scheduled course was canceled, then another, so my mother requested something else to do. If there weren't any students to tend to, then perhaps she could help with bookkeeping. On days Simon was in the office she stood by as he rifled through his briefcase gathering receipts. On days he was traveling she slunk upstairs to stare at empty beds and wonder why floors in rooms that hadn't been occupied in weeks creaked more, even through carpet tile.

When a young man from South Africa arrived at Intracare, he spoke excitedly to my father of his ambitions to co-author a radio training curriculum he could take back with him to Johannesburg via a network of vocational schools called City & Guilds. Doc Vick had a white father and an Indian mother, and a pretty Portuguese wife he had met at Bible college and married in defiance of antimiscegenation laws. My father agreed to help Doc because he liked him, and he could easily picture South African youth lining up for their course certificates, eager to see how high they could rise in a post-Apartheid country, which, they hoped, would happen any day now—

Doc Vick and my father worked for months, then submitted the complete proposal to Simon and to Hans, a Swiss-born engineer whose agreeableness had made him Simon's de facto deputy. Simon said *thank you, Stan* and they would take it from there. Really, they ought to wait for the new TWR logo before submitting it for City & Guilds accreditation, and that was still a work in progress. *Why wait?* Better, really. The new logo was better. *But that's ridiculous.* Papers were shuffled, deadlines passed.

My father acquires bulk when angry. His shoulders swell from the effort to contain his upset. Then he exhales and is shorter than before. Doc returned to work for TWR Swaziland and the season changed, the thermostat clicked, nothing was accomplished, and my mother began to worry about dust. Less vacuuming was good but unused rooms still got dusty.

✦

Wes and Viv came to visit—they'd never been to Europe before—and arrived just in time for Simon's fixation on Proverbs 26:11, shared during a Tuesday staff meeting. *As a dog returns to his vomit, so a fool returns to his folly.* He wanted all Intracare staffers to bear this verse in mind, because he was very concerned that the inferior quality of most missionary radio programming fatally compromised the medium's potential. The staff at Intracare, and TWR more generally, was in the trenches. They were responsible. Would they keep on producing the same old mediocre stuff, expecting better results? Think, he urged. Think of the Iron and Bamboo Curtains. How could anyone raised under the thumb of India's caste system hear and truly understand the freedom described in the Gospel? What were the odds that a Japanese teenager would defy family and peer pressure and go to a Christian church? What about the Muslim Aceh of North Sumatra?

Simon looked around at his staff. It was imperative that Christian views be floated in the "marketplace of ideas" where they could compete with New Ageism and such, and perhaps TWR ought to start thinking about:

- Contextualizing
- Market research
- Phone-in programs
- Interviews with people in crisis, sort of a "man on the street" type of thing

This was so important, Simon stressed, because bad programming placed a strain upon the sovereignty of God. But it was hard to find the right people. That was a major, major, major concern of his—how difficult it was to find qualified people.

My father presented some of his feelings about this speech to Wes. Wes told my father he'd just have to wait and see what happened. Meanwhile, he could pray. Maybe it was good for us to know that there were people who thought badly of us, our work, our abilities. Accusations of incompetence kept us humble.

So my father stifled the unchristian urge to raise his hand during staff meetings and ask Simon what he liked best about flying Singapore Airlines.

✦

Blessed are the peacemakers: for they shall be called the children of God. My father struggled with this. People liked talking about peace. People everywhere were all for it. They can just imagine how wonderful peace would be. *Imagine?* As if our default state were peace. This was not true of infants. Not true of toddlers, teenagers, parents who have to work late.

Press a little harder as to how these secular advocates of peace proposed to bring it about and you mainly hear facile stuff about having more respect for differences. Press harder still and people speak of compromise. But the sons of God are compromisers? mediators?

If peacemakers are blessed, then perhaps peace did not

function as most people imagined. Say, for instance, you urged compromise in a conflict between a jerk (who was demanding something he had no right to demand in the first place) and someone kind. That compromise would encourage the mean and discourage the gentle. Compromise and mediation in and of themselves are morally neutral.

So maybe—I imagine my father thinking around this time— peace was best thought of in terms of what peace was not. Maybe its opposite was not warring but stubbornness. Perhaps peace was an ability to surrender.

He began to realize he didn't have that ability, had never had it, and wasn't sure he wanted it.

Then Mrs. Luverne Berg, one of our Minneapolis supporters, sent him a letter in which she reminded him of what Thomas à Kempis had to say about being treated poorly. À Kempis maintained that every instance of someone being a jackass was an opportunity to turn toward God. We ought to so firmly focus on God, in fact, that we experience human encouragement as mere cake decoration, and its opposite merely as a welcome reminder of our dependence on Him. Luverne also sent, per my father's request, a copy of Dietrich Bonhoeffer's *Letters and Papers from Prison*. (He couldn't find it the American Book Shop in Amsterdam.) The volume contained lines like this, written by Bonhoeffer to his parents on May 15, 1943: "In 100 years it will all be over." The words were not his; a previous occupant of his prison cell had scribbled them over the cell door. A great deal could be said about that sentence, Bonhoeffer contemplated. "The great thing is to stick to what one still has and can do—there is still plenty left—and not to be dominated by the thought of what one cannot do, and by feelings of resentment and discontent."

✦

LATER   "Could have been his background," my father said.

We were discussing possible biographical reasons for Simon's management style. Status anxiety was one idea.

"He grew up Brethren, you know, so—"

"No. What does that mean?"

"Well, they were kinda out of the mainstream. They worshipped in gospel halls, they were typically lower class. Given how extremely class-conscious Britain is . . . They were seen as hicks, you know. Simon was very intelligent but Brethren boys didn't matriculate at Oxford. He probably felt he should have but—you know. Tough yuck."

"Ah."

"He was really gifted. He valued the cut-and-thrust of academic debate. I think he felt unrecognized. He was always trying to prove that he belonged."

✦

We held on to a sense of ourselves by repeating family stories. My mother's tales all focused on peculiar near misses:

1. How she and her brother Paul had to wash dishes together, one soaping and the other rinsing and drying, and he'd brandish the carving knife like a sword and threaten to kill her. Now Paul commanded the U.S. Navy base in Brindisi.

2. How David, the eldest brother, the one who became a pediatrician, made her play Iron Lung one summer. The game consisted of her lying very still in a cardboard box in the basement for hours until he declared her miraculously cured.

3. She was once persuaded—by Paul—that her doll's hair would grow back if she cut it. That doll had been her only Christmas present, and it was bald by December 26. She remained bald because they couldn't afford a wig.

4. How a school friend's father owned the Cambridge Theatre, but the Johnson kids weren't allowed to go to the movies, none of them was. So my mom and her friend sat on the stoop behind the theater and just ate the free popcorn. And there they sat in their dresses and lace-trimmed anklets and ate popcorn while inside children whose parents did not have such high standards watched *Lady and the Tramp*.

5. Then that time Orville and Marian were getting ready to have the First Baptist Church deacons over for pie one Sunday when Wayne Turner showed up to kill Marian. Actually— no. Orville wasn't there. Anyhow, Minnesota, circa 1956, here's what happened:

Wayne Turner and Marian had had run-ins before because he had been quite adamant about his desire to join the First Baptist choir upon his release from prison. But Marian suspected his motives and said so. He retaliated by placing an ad in the Chisholm newspaper that stated Mrs. Orville Johnson was looking for nude dancers to perform at a party she was throwing.

One Sunday afternoon when Orville was still at church and all the kids were upstairs and Marian was putting a pie in the oven, Wayne enters the house through the unlocked back porch, up the linoleum steps—one, two, three—and he's in the kitchen with a revolver in his hand.

"Oh hi!" Marian says, as if Wayne Turner habitually breezed through the back door like that. "I wasn't expecting you." She sees the gun. She offers Wayne blueberry pie.

("It wasn't going in the oven then." "No. There were multiple pies.")

Then: the sound of Orville and the deacons pulling up in the gravel driveway. No shots were fired. Hallelujah.

The sad PS was that Wayne Turner proceeded to skip town and murder two people at a Louisiana gas station. The young woman who drove the getaway car was the First Baptist Church Sunday school teacher who wore red lipstick. She was pregnant and may or may not have ended up in prison.

(So when telling this story, hit the nude dancers bit again at the end. Oh, and also mention that the Johnson kids got police escorts to school for the rest of the year, so that was nice.)

✦

My father was quieter during these childhood memory conversations. He smirked, he hemmed and harrumphed, he walked in and out of the room, different paperbacks in his hand each time. We urged him to participate. C'mon Da-ad.

He didn't remember much from his childhood, he'd say. But in time he settled upon this story: Three boys in the house, a lot of cereal being eaten. They plowed through boxes of Rice Krispies. And one time General Mills ran a promotion whereby if you mailed in x number of proofs of purchase, they'd send you a plastic ring with Snap, Crackle, or Pop on it. So he eagerly cut out the necessary proofs of purchase and Vivian helped him place the correct stamps on the envelope and he waited. He must have been around seven, he said. The ring finally arrived and he wore Crackle to class the next day. After school three bullies ran up from behind and pushed him facedown into a snowbank and stole it. He got up, brushed the snow from his pants legs, picked up his wet mittens, and cried all the way home.

That was it? we asked. That was the story?

He nodded. Yep. That was it.

We scrunched up our noses as if someone had brought in a platter of egg salad sandwiches. He preferred telling stories about his former students back in those suburban Minnesota high schools. *There was a boy who killed flies like a ninja*, he said. One girl raised her hand and asked *Mr. Huesstadd, may I pleazzze go to the bathroom?* every. single. day. So once, when he heard the familiar *may I pleazzze* he said no. No, she may not. *Then I'm gonna pee right here in my pants*, she said. Go right ahead, he said. This was the moral: Girl did not pee her pants. Some people just liked to see what they could get away with, and they usually did this by requesting things they didn't even want. It was your job—possibly even your Christian duty—to call these people's bluff. Then there was that day he glimpsed—mimeographed announcement on bulletin board—the word "co-curricular" to describe school sports. Used to be these were "extracurricular" activities.

"Practically Orwellian," he said. Then he had to explain

to us all, except Amy, who had read *1984* in 1984, because it seemed the right thing to do, what "Orwellian" meant.

He also talked about how teachers in the United States were not allowed to flunk a student for not showing up to class, and how he strenuously objected when the principal first announced this policy. The principal asked him if he wanted to go to jail for the privilege of flunking some squirrelly kid. Yes, my father said. Yes he did.

✦

EMAILS, 2013   Me: In other news, I was remembering that time—1983—when I was horsing around on Laura's staircase in that old Victorian and accidentally sent a loose baluster flying . . . which landed on Mom's head. Do you remember this? Talking to me about it afterward?

Amy: . . . Quite honestly, I thought I was the one who kicked it out!

Me: It was me. Definitely.

Amy: Really? Are you 100% sure? I take full responsibility. And full responsibility for trying to put it on you.

Me: 100% sure.

Amy: Well, if you still want to put it on me, I'm happy to take it. Love you tons, A.

✦

Day-to-day life blurred into routines of homework, rain, and setting the table. Were it not for a trip to London, 1986 could easily be forgotten.

There were advantages to traveling under cover of God-fearing. The Foreign Missions Club was fashioned out of three conjoined row houses at 20–26 Aberdeen Park, a leafy block in Highbury Islington in north London. The walls between what had once been single-family houses had been knocked down, but most of the room arrangements remained as in the original dwellings. The wallpaper was textured and staircase treads well worn. The club had been founded in 1893 to provide low-cost lodging to missionaries and missionary sympathizers traipsing through town for one reason or the other. It now smelled of damp woolens and the insides of cookie tins after all the shortbread had been eaten. The old offices of the China Inland Mission, which may have been involved in sending Eric Liddell of *Chariots of Fire* fame to his fate—we'd have to check on that when we got to a bookstore, my father said—were a few blocks away.

The porcelain cups were chipped. At the bottom of the staircase opposite the front entrance was a coin-operated hot water dispensing machine, and nailed to the wall beside it a rack of packets containing cocoa and instant coffee. I liked this setup. To be able to obtain hot cocoa without speaking to anyone first was amazing. London was obviously where interesting things happened to interesting children. From the evidence presented in *Ballet Shoes* and *Theater Shoes* and *The Lion, the Witch, and the Wardrobe*, the ideal original situation for misunderstood children was a drafty London home liberally stocked with umbrellas and dust, either just before or immediately after World War II. In a gray, big city it was easier to believe that feeling out of sorts was the essence of the human condition. Here we could believe that not fitting in was the lot of the best girls everywhere.

By the second breakfast at the Foreign Missions Club, Mom remarked that baked beans on toast was *a real challenge*. But a gong was rung to announce breakfast, and in the low-ceilinged breakfast room on the ground floor, we found seats at the same table we had sat at the previous day, and this, I thought, was terrific. Plates of buttered white toast were delivered and tea poured, just as it was yesterday, the aluminum teapot left on the table so we could pour our own refills. The baked beans were also on a buffet table at the opposite end of the room and therefore not strictly necessary—we could avoid them if we wanted to, I beseeched my mom wordlessly, so we were really doing okay.

Our next-to-last night at the Foreign Missions Club, our parents went to a musical adaptation *of Mutiny on the Bounty*, starring George C. Scott, which Dad in particular was excited about because George C. Scott was Patton, so to speak. Amy and Dad had already seen *Evita* while Mom and I went to *The Mousetrap*. Plenty of new paperbacks had been purchased at Foyle's on Charing Cross Road—a street we dimly perceived as significant—so we'd be spending the night in.

Amy and I lolled around on the twin beds in our parents' room while they got ready. Upon leaving they instructed us to alert a staff member in the event of fire or bodily injury. Amy rolled her eyes. The door shut. She looked at me. It was obvious that we needed to put on Laura Ashley dresses and lip balm bought at the Body Shop on Covent Garden and run. Amy's dress: white sailor collar above a wash of pastels lifted from Monet's *Waterlilies*, cinched at the waist, ample fabric falling to midcalf. Mine: pale lavender delicately patterned with pink posies and peaches. Up every staircase and down every staircase. We would enter every unlocked room and sit on every unoccupied chair. Our pale skirts would billow up as we collapsed into faded chintz seats. We would go-go-go until we were out of breath, or had thoroughly convinced ourselves that we were beautiful or enviable, or both.

✦

By our fourth fundraising furlough, Amy and I, emboldened by nice Laura Ashley dresses, discover dramatic irony. After the post-slide-show mingling and smiling and punch, kindly old men in polyester blend jackets leaned in to ask the question:

"So, are you going to be a missionary when you grow up?"

"No." A beat. Snickery smiles. "No way."

MORE THAN CONQUERORS

Because once you knew the answers you were expected to give, it was hard to have to deliver them. That same summer I was sent to Trinity Lutheran church camp and handed a stapled booklet of dittoed pages and instructed to hang on to it because we'd be filling it out throughout the week. On the cover were crude drawings of a heart ("God is love"), sun ("God is full of compassion every morning"), coffee cup ("God is my portion"), rainbow ("God is faithful"), and birthday present ("God is good"). Inside were workbook-like exercises. *Find the key verbs, adjectives, and adverbs in Lamentations 3:21–26*, for example.

And a QUESTION: What is something you would like to do today at camp?

I put "swim" on the first line and filled the rest with *? ? ? ?*

Then ACTIVITIES: Read Acts 12. Draw a comic strip of Peter in jail. Write captions of how he felt. Do a report for TV or radio about Peter's escape.

Then, consider this QUESTION: How does Jesus's promise to his disciples ("And surely I am with you always, to the very end of the age") apply to you?

In the RESPONSE section I wrote: *Jesus will be with you all the time. And that you never have to be afraid when your [sic] alone. Bla-bla-bla-bla-bla-bla-bla-bla-bla-bla-bla-bla-bla (the end).*

*Bla-bla-bla*s because easy answer. Also because small comfort. Why would it be necessary to know God was with you, were you not ever on the verge of an accident? By the booklet's last page—the GOD IS GOOD section—I had stopped filling in the blanks.

✦

LATER   Me: "What happened at Intracare?"

My father: "Well, eventually I got the sense that it would not matter if I showed up for work or not."

Amy, meanwhile, had developed conviction. Books by Simone de Beauvoir appeared on her nightstand. She learned that taking the bus to Paris was cheap and biking hurriedly to the station at 5:45 a.m. Saturdays to catch it was exhilarating, as was regaining your normal heart rate sitting amid travelers with whom you shared nothing but a destination and that destination was Paris. Unless an elderly woman had accidentally locked herself in the WC at the rest stop outside Brussels, they would be at the Place de la Concorde by 12:30 or 1:00. The bus driver stood, stretched, and scratched his middle-aged paunch while informing his passengers that if they weren't back on the bus by midnight sharp, he'd leave without them.

"Be *care-fuul*. You don't want to spend the night in Pigalle." He winked as Amy and her friend Marieke, always in thick black eyeliner, filed past.

They disembarked into midday Paris and felt sun on their hair and his stare on their asses. But taking a tour bus was all right if you wore scarves and would be smoking Gauloises as soon as you managed to commandeer a café table. A photograph taken around this time shows sixteen-year-old Amy looking directly at the camera, knowingness teasing the corners of her smile. Her eyes had turned a blue so icy it made her gaze cradle insinuations without her even trying. She was still learning to control her stare's unnerving effect when she decided that church on Sunday was a thing of her past, and this is how cheap day-trips to Paris helped a lot. Getting home at 6:30 Sunday a.m. made it easier to avoid the inevitable why-I-don't-want-to-go-to-church conversations. Everyone could pretend that all she wanted on those mornings was more sleep.

During the week Amy agreed with her school friends that there was something crazy imperialist about the way the German TV dubbed all English-language programs, so you'd see *Dynasty*'s Joan Collins and Linda Evans wrestling, their screeching and heavy breathing and hair pulling all in German, and then next thing you knew you'd be imagining some poor German lady in a TV studio standing at a microphone having to make those huffing puffing sex noises. After class she and her friends biked over to the Hoekje, a coffee shop around the corner and down the block from the train station. There they admired their young hands as they cradled cups of coffee with milk. Nobody else's parents were Christian. Sometimes they studied but good intentions quickly cooled and mostly they felt themselves bright and full of potential. They made sarcastic remarks in hushed tones yet sensed that sarcasm was perhaps too easy. They aspired to something beyond sarcasm but trusted they'd get there eventually if they only stayed cool.

At home Amy stopped giving any more information than strictly asked for. She kept her answers clipped, sheared down.

My mother, too. She discovered a book called *Color Me Beautiful*, which divided the world's population into four categories based on what color clothing they looked best in. People whose skin had blue undertones, for instance, glowed in certain hues but appeared sullen and blotchy in other shades. Yellow-undertoned people should not be wearing the same colors as blue-undertoned people. It was important that you knew which one you were.

"When I was a young girl, I wanted so much to be pretty," author Carole Jackson wrote. "While the powder blue uniform required at my school made some of the girls look great, it did nothing for me. It in fact made me look gray, dull, and lifeless. The color of that daily uniform robbed me of some potentially good feelings about myself well into adult life. Discovering lipstick and rouge as a teenager brought me instant life, but it was not until years later that I discovered the real magic of color. MY colors . . . the missing link to finding my best self."

Missionary women also needed help locating their best selves, my mother decided. Modest clothing budgets couldn't be helped, but when combing the thrift store racks, at least they could pick out items that didn't make them look awful. Once she'd purchased the scarf set needed to conduct color analysis sessions at home, she extended an invitation to the women of Intracare. They sat ankles crossed facing the sun and held a large round white-framed mirror in their laps as my mother draped a series of solid-colored scarves over their necks and shoulders, framing their faces. Signs of the right shades were radiance, sparkling eyes, robust cheeks. The wrong shades? The sunken appearance of wallflowers and old maids. "Better 1 or better 2?" is how my mother worked, like an optometrist working toward a prescription.

LOOK AT THE FACE, NOT AT THE COLOR—those were the book's instructions.

I stood watching these tutorials because they took place in my room. Southern exposure, second floor, it had the best light in the house. I was also being helpful, my mother assured me and the woman in the chair—in my memory it's always Caroline Wigley, the Intracare secretary—because an extra set of eyes lessened the chance of individual preference influencing the "better 1 or better 2" calls.

There was still the question of whether this fixation on looking good was okay, spiritually speaking. My mother decided that it was, because it involved working with what God had given us. It also helped you save money. A strong inner conviction about what shades she looked best in allowed a woman to let seasonal color trends pass her by without regret. "Oh, that's not my color," you'd simply say, and no one would think twice about it. My mother handed out "Shades of Beauty" color swatch booklets designed to be kept in purses at all times to help prevent the purchase of wrong-colored blouses. She was supposed to charge for them—this was supposed to be a home business, at least for some—but she couldn't bring herself to do so. Charging would have exposed the desire beneath, the desire to escape from virtue.

Before bed I practiced a new conviction: that it was a sign of weakness to rely on a bookmark to tell you where you'd left off. Strength was found in committing page numbers to memory. So I stared at the number in the upper right corner of the page where I'd stopped reading and whispered it over and over: *80, 80, 80, 80, 80, 80, 80, 80, 80, 80, 80*. Exhale. *80, 80, 80, 80, 80, 80, 80, 80*. If I whispered firmly and noticed how the paper yellowed around the 80, how black the ink, then I could set the book down. If I couldn't recall 80 when I picked up the book the next night, I flipped between familiar and unfamiliar passages until I perceived the dividing line but also knew, at the same time, that I really had to be better.

✦

Then it was over. My father knew the Intracare experiment was coming to an end when the course schedule for the next session was announced. This one would focus on Russia and the Soviet bloc. Simon was aware that my father had studied some Russian history, had taken Russian language classes, and had been keenly looking forward to this particular course. He wanted to help the Russians design new programs that would speak to the reality of their situation better than programs like *Unshackled* had. The teaching schedule was determined by Simon and announced via neatly typed assignment schedules distributed through interoffice mail.

So my father had that interoffice envelope on his desk, and this is how I envision the moment when he could no longer deny that he'd been broken:

First, position the envelope carefully so that it lined up straight along both length and width of his desk. This took ten minutes. Then he looked across the room at Caroline Wigley, thin-lipped, sensibly attired, determined to remain oblivious. For kicks he imagined that Caroline was a CIA plant. He stared out the window at the hedgerow and silently declared hedges the

French poodles of the plant kingdom—clipped, emasculated, sad. But he had delayed the sting long enough. He pulled the course schedule from the envelope and saw his name nowhere. Pronounced like Higgins from *Magnum, P.I.*, that reality might sound better. He tried it under his breath. *I'm sorry, sir. Your name is not on the list.*

A few weeks later Simon Osmund was summoned to TWR headquarters to be formally presented with some questions about his leadership. The scriptures laid out a series of steps for confronting someone. Matthew 18:15–17: *Moreover if your brother sins against you, go and tell him his fault between you and him alone. If he hears you, you have gained your brother. But if he will not hear, take with you one or two more, that "by the mouth of two or three witnesses every word may be established." And if he refuses to hear them, tell it to the church.*

I imagine TWR top brass seated around a table. First concern to address was whether he'd been sufficiently thrifty. Second, had he paid too little attention to Intracare amid his other duties? Third, did not Intracare employ able men and women who would gladly have made up the deficit had Simon only delegated better? Might he have been less the sergeant major, more the servant leader? Did they question his sincerity? If Simon truly believed the job before him was holy and good, then he would not have acted so cavalierly. He would have felt his staff's suffering keenly.

The Intracare staff did not receive any indication as to how this meeting went until the following Monday, when Simon showed up aftershaved and whistling. The following week my parents were informed via Telex to expect a letter from TWR executive Jack Hicks at TWR headquarters in New Jersey. Here are its best lines:

> I realize that there has, in fact, been a "withering process" which
> has transpired as it relates to Stan.

I am not sure that I can put my finger on the "why" of all of this.

Your openness, your honesty, your caring about people all comes through.

On paper, when talking about it in Bonaire, it all seemed very right.

Why didn't it work in Holland? I am not sure, but I can say part of it no doubt falls under the category of personal relationships . . . Somehow it seems that [Simon] has never been able to give you the amount of attention, care and concern that perhaps you needed. This is despite the commitments on both of your parts to "make it work."

I believe another factor is the difference in perception of the quality of the output of your work. On one hand perhaps [Simon's] expectations were too great. Also, your high expectations for your own achievements have been a constant point of tension and frustration.

Please don't misunderstand what I am saying. I am not at all implying that you have not done any meaningful, good work. I am talking about the preponderance of investment of your time, which by your own admission has felt unnecessarily low.

While in India and Sri Lanka, I was not looking for any particular answer or solution to your situation.

After a considerable amount of prayer and discussion, I feel led to indicate to you that there would be a meaningful job available in the Ministry Department of our South Asian Field.

The school system in Sri Lanka is very excellent in the English language. In fact, there are several higher education options for our children.

I am sure this will hit you as something coming out of the blue.

May I suggest that you be in touch with Eddie [Perera] for more details? I would ask Eddie to also include opportunities for Karen as well as Stan. I know, for example, they may be looking for someone in the area of bookkeeping.

My parents did not think that relocating to Sri Lanka was the answer they were looking for. Hadn't the whole point of Intracare been to stem the spread of pale, awkward families from the American Midwest into such places? My father replied:

> Thanks for your letter. I do hope that we can continue to be friends. I have always considered you a friend. It was out of that friendship that I made certain commitments. Do I feel betrayed? Betrayal is a strong word. Isolated? Yes. Abandoned? Perhaps. Subject to leadership negligence? Yes.
>
> It is obvious that [Simon] and I clashed as personalities. But this must be considered in the light of the fact that I am basically a passive person; quite tolerant of different styles and perspectives. For a clash to happen, the issues are probably deeper than style, culture, or perspective. The issue of assessing the quality of my work is another point you made. My own assessment may be irrelevant. Unfortunately there are few individuals in TWR who are qualified to judge us in our broadcasting, teaching, and managerial skills. I will, however, be more than happy to have them evaluated by the community at large and in the marketplace, if necessary.
>
> We are not considering the Sri Lanka position. It is probably not appropriate and the timing is certainly not. I promised you that I would go without causing you any trouble. We intend to keep our word. Our resignation from Trans World Radio effective at the end of our term will be coming under separate cover to the appropriate people.

That elicited a measured response from another TWR executive. The Lord had brought us to mind on occasion, he alleged, and he had been praying for us. "Although it is not easy to see you leave Trans World Radio, I have to believe that the Lord has given you that direction."

Twenty-seven years in evangelical work had him nearly convinced that Satan targeted certain people, he continued, and while my parents had legitimate reasons to be discouraged, he hoped they could make the next six months their very best.

A final letter on the subject from Jack Hicks stated that the Stan and Karen he knew were not quitters. He felt that Sri Lanka was a legitimate area of ministry. And granted, the Holland assignment had been a less happy experience than everyone had hoped.

But many positive things were accomplished, he felt, "and I am sure God has taught you many good lessons. Therefore, I do not feel this time can be looked on as a failure either." It was signed, "Your friend in Christ."

✦

All I can remember about departure this time, aside from one Saturday morning errand when my father handed me five guilders and gave instructions to stop by the Free Record Store after grocery shopping and buy the 7-inch single of the Talking Heads' "Road to Nowhere," is that we were cautiously optimistic. My father had discovered the song upon strolling into the den while Amy and I sat slack-jawed watching *Countdown* with Adam Curry. He stood mesmerized.

"Who's this?" he asked.

"What?"

"The band. This thing, this video, this thing we're watching now."

"It's the Talking Heads," Amy said.

"The what?"

"The Talking Heads."

"Who are they?"

"I dunno. They're from the States."

I thought he stayed to watch because this was one of the few music videos in which no one was pantsless and straddling a sofa or motorcycle or a person of the opposite sex, and so he felt comfortable observing it in our company. But it was the lyrics. We knew—sorta—where we were going, but not exactly where we'd been. It was okay, though, this road to nowhere we were on. Whether my father heard in these lines an analysis of his own situation or a surprising self-diagnosis from those in the business of churning out music videos—he had just read Neil Postman's *Amusing Ourselves to Death*—I have no idea.

Mainly I—age twelve—thought Dad's sudden interest in pop music was a sign of progress. We started packing up our belongings and felt the satisfaction of being good at this. The process of holding an object in the hand and asking a series of questions: What box does this go in? With what other stuff? What will we write on the outside of the box? Where's the marker? Will we open this box across the ocean, start unwrapping objects grown mysterious for having been out of sight for several weeks, and think *ugh*, what were we hoping this would do for us?

No one felt like cooking so we wound up at a cheap Indonesian restaurant located off a highway exit. It was practically deserted. We took a table next to the window and ate without pleasure. After our plates were cleared, a hostess sauntered over with a red plastic Coca-Cola tray on which were arranged hard candies, mints, and loose cigarettes. My mother selected a cigarette and leaned in to the lighter that the hostess, who had yet to say a word in Dutch or English, held out for her.

My jaw dropped. She coughed, cleared her throat, and exhaled smoke out of the side of her mouth as her eyes fixed outside on the parking lot, empty save for our Mitsubishi and sparrows fighting over a clump of rice that had escaped a trash bag.

"You smoke?"

She grimaced. "Well—" She tried to wave away the smoke that bounced off the window back into her eyes.

"You *smoke*?"

"No. No. Not in years. I mean, probably not since Grand Junction, Iowa. Since my early twenties."

I looked to Amy. Amy just stared at her lap. I looked to my father. He looked like he wanted to place his head under a tire.

My mother's eyes sparkled. She winked at me.

But her rebellion was over as quickly as it began. As she stubbed out the half-smoked cigarette, her expression clouded over. She grabbed her purse, lifted her gaze, and that was our signal. It was time to go again.

✦

Anyone who goes anywhere, moves anywhere, who absorbs a new idea, is hoping:

This _____ will be a homecoming. Will feel like another two inches of height. Like lowering bare feet into water the perfect temperature.

✦

For my father the move was a defeat, a rejection, but even that was a sort of homecoming—the stories of his father, and his father's father, came out to meet him. One evening many years later he confesses he wonders how the tune might have played differently if good fathers weren't so hard to find or—as in his father's father's case—so prematurely dead.

INTERLUDE: ORIGIN MYTHS

After having ten children baptized at his town's Lutheran church, Paul Hustad stopped to hear a traveling tent preacher one night and cried. He did not excel at crying but it felt good. This Baptist preacher persuaded Paul, who actually needed little persuading, that he ought to be "born again." So he was.

In fact Paul had long suspected that the Lutheran church was not serving his family sufficiently nourishing food. Some Sundays he didn't even follow the sermon. Did the dried-out husk of a man in the pulpit know anything of deep feeling? He had listened to shop owners extol the virtues of ten-pound sacks of flour with more passion.

It was obvious what needed to happen next. He would build a chapel on the edge of his acreage and let it be known that traveling Baptist preachers who wanted to hold convocations in this chapel were welcome. The chapel would not be pretentious or elaborate—simply a modest framed structure with benches that sat a couple dozen souls, with room for overflow and latecomers at the back. In any event he was done with Lutherans.

That not everyone in Yellow Medicine County was impressed by this enterprise came as a mild surprise to Paul. He felt harsh eyes on his shoulder blades. More worrisome than gossip, however, was the matter of his children's marriage prospects. Who would marry these heresy-prone Hustads? Once-promising prospects backed away, hand over heart and mouthing regrets. It caused his wife, Anna, great anxiety.

Indeed it was a complication he had failed to consider, and this failure to anticipate trouble led him to wonder. Not that he would have acted differently given the opportunity to think differently.

Because God knew best. He learned of Boone Biblical College and Associated Institutions and decided to send his eldest boys there, for a few months at least. There they could deepen their understanding of the Gospel and maybe meet some God-fearing girls. Three of the four did exactly that, and Paul considered this proof that God was good.

His son Peter met a young Wisconsin woman named Clara. She grew up on a farm and had briefly worked as a maid for some fancy Madison families. They were married and moved to be near Peter's family in southwestern Minnesota. One evening after supper, October 1919, he wiped his mouth on his sleeve and pushed his chair back from the table. Quick kiss for Clara, baby Donald, too, and with that he snatched his hat and rifle and hurried out the door to meet up with two cousins who lived on the adjacent farm.

The three of them reached Thorson's slough near Battle Lake in ten quick minutes and stationed themselves in the late autumn grass and watched the sky. At the sound of the first flock of ducks, the youngest cousin—another Peter, Peter E.—turned too quickly and lost his footing. His gun discharged as his ankle twisted.

"Whoa, there. Steady now!" he announced, straightening himself. Then he realized that a significant portion of his namesake's face lay spattered in the grass.

"He saw his cousin fall but did not realize what had happened to him until he went over to help him to his feet, when it was discovered a part of his head had been blown off," the

Granite Falls Advocate reported a few days later. The third cousin on the scene, Edwin, appears briefly in the newspaper story to restrain the shooter from turning the gun on himself. Peter was twenty-four years old, and in the previous year three of his siblings—aged fifteen, thirteen, and two—had succumbed to influenza.

The idea that this was no accident was floated around town but quickly shushed. There was little point to that kind of speculating, and as Clara's second baby was on the way, surely she had other things to fret about. Clara moved in with Paul and Anna, and Wes was born six months later into a house brimming with people and yet not full. Too many arms and limbs and yet not as many as there might have been had God's mercy taken different form, or if Paul had not suffered an accident that compelled them to take a house in town, running the farm now physically impossible for him. Still they kept a milk cow and some chickens, and Paul hobbled around with a cane and prayed in Norwegian, wishing he could still do useful work.

And there was Clara, with her toddler and screaming baby, and she felt herself getting plumper by the week because she ate nervously and on the day toddler Don tumbled down the basement steps and lay there motionless on the floor, not breathing for a few endless dread seconds even after she picked him up, Anna came over to tut-tut and say, loud enough for everyone in the kitchen to hear, that maybe it would have been better if the boy hadn't survived.

A letter from Clara's sister Lillie urged her to the sheltering arms of Boone Biblical College. *Come back*, Lillie wrote in 1921. She and the boys might even stay for free. Lillie would speak to Mr. Crawford, the director, about Clara's situation.

Besides, Lillie intimated, it wasn't as if Clara had a wealth of options. Returning to her family in Wisconsin was never considered, at least not on paper.

Boone Biblical College was not a college. Classes were held but essentially one arrived at Boone when one had nowhere else to go. The campus had separate residence halls for girls, boys, adults, seniors, and infants. Because Mr. Crawford prized self-sufficiency, he had also overseen the construction of a church sanctuary, elementary school, high school, dry goods store, cannery, bakery, laundry, and print shop. Every able-bodied resident was expected to help bring in the harvest on the parcel of farmland Mr. Crawford owned on the edge of town. So Clara and her boys made the three-hundred-mile trip south, staying briefly in a Main Street apartment where miners and railroad workers boarded. When Mr. Crawford decided she had waited long enough, she moved herself and her boys into a single room in the college's main residence hall. Clara threw her hat onto the bed, sat down, shook out her long brown hair, and waited to see what would happen next. She was given a pair of thick dark tights to cover her legs.

When the boys remembered Boone many years later, they remembered the clacking sound produced by black-heeled Sunday shoes racing down empty institutional hallways. They had the run of the place. Other children lived at the BBC, but only in the boys' and girls' dorms, and those kids were functionally orphans, which is to say their exact situation regarding parents dead or alive was not always clear, but no one wanted them, in any event. Wes and Don attracted attention not only because they lived in the adult residence hall but because their mother was around, albeit prohibited from singling them out for affection whenever they ate or worshipped in the common areas.

At night Clara tossed fitfully. Asleep, she moaned and murmured, crying out until one of the boys, usually Don, scrambled over and shook her shoulder until she woke from her nightmares and apologized. Once the boys were old enough they moved to the room next door but still heard her wailing through the wall.

But the next morning it was always back to work and

potatoes, turnips, tomatoes, corn, beans, beets, carrots, radishes, and lettuce. Vegetables and salads, chewy white bread and rice pudding. Maybe meat gravy on Sunday—that they remembered fondly. On Fridays, canned salmon. The pain of canned salmon suppers was alleviated somewhat by the other Friday happening: Walter Damrosch's *Music Appreciation Hour*. Teachers tuned classroom radios to NBC, broadcasting an actual symphony orchestra live from New York City. Then music lessons and Bible memorization and in the afternoon, depending on the season, laying up hay in the barn.

In the evenings, Don ran around the fields arms flung wide to get cows into the barn for the evening milking. He'd be up again at 4:30 for the morning milking.

On birthdays and Christmases, Wes and Don and Clara enjoyed eating apart from the communal tables in a room to themselves. Clara would arrange a treat of Parker House rolls and beef gravy, so delicious it moistened their eyes and prompted the boys to wonder whether good food eaten daily would still taste heavenly or quickly lose its flavor.

Clara did receive offers of remarriage, and not all of them from homeless men. Surely some of those fellows would have sufficed, her sons felt. But no. When Boone Biblical College and Associated Institutions received a radio operator's license for ten-watt KFGQ, she wrote scripts for on-air meditations about God's relationship with His children, Psalms 91:4: *He shall cover thee with His feathers and under His wings shalt thou trust* and 2 Timothy 2:19: *The Lord knoweth them that are His* among her favorite verses. The studio was in the basement and they could see the transmitter tower from their residence hall window.*

---

*The radio operator's license issued to Lois Crawford, Dr. Crawford's daughter, was the first one issued to a woman. Many small religious organizations were early to embrace radio. The first broadcast license granted a religious group went to the Church of the Covenant in Washington, D.C., in December 1921. Calvary Baptist Church of New York City received its radio license a few weeks later. "I shall try to continue doing my part,"

Don was kicked out of BBC for paying too much attention to a young woman. Mr. Crawford informed Don he was going to hell. The year was 1935. Wes's melancholy grew edges.

Don's anger at Clara for not coming to his defense in the face of Crawford's condemnation blocked his remembering what she looked like. For years his brain refused to conjure up the image of her face.

---

pastor John Roach Stratton remarked, "tearing down the strongholds of Satan. And I hope that our radio system will prove so efficient that when I twist the Devil's tail in New York, his squawk will be heard across the continent."

More license requests followed, and increasingly from low-lying towns and more cash-poor organizations. In 1927 the FRC was created to impose some order on the process. Before the FRC, nearby radio stations might opt for the same frequency and jam each other's signal. A station might broadcast at 1220AM one day and 1400AM the next. Any kook who could afford the equipment could air any variety of gospel they pleased—socialists and syndicalists as well as the Jesus-minded.

Aimee Semple McPherson, the proprietress of KSFG in Los Angeles, did not take kindly to regulation. She sent a telegram to then Chamber of Commerce secretary Herbert Hoover requesting that he

PLEASE ORDER YOUR MINIONS OF SATAN TO LEAVE MY STATION ALONE STOP YOU CANNOT EXPECT THE ALMIGHTY TO ABIDE BY YOUR WAVE LENGTH NONSENSE STOP.

In 1929 the FRC ceased issuing new radio operators' licenses to religious and other special interest groups. They would have to persuade existing stations to air their programs for them. As the Great Depression dragged on, this arrangement didn't seem so bad—even a modest 250-watt transmitter staffed by volunteers cost money.

What was the best way to get a program on someone else's station? Opinions were split. One side believed the FRC should set aside frequencies for noncommercial public access channels, which would dole out time slots to worthy applicants. The other camp maintained that such "public broadcasting" was tantamount to restricting commerce. Commercial radio stations proposed instead that they allocate a few free hours here and there for programming in the public interest. These time slots were called "sustaining time," and in 1933 they became FRC policy.

Evangelical programmers now had two options: (1) Sunday morning time slots, which most successful broadcasters were happy to slough off anyhow, or (2) Buy airtime. Many preferred to do that.

Major national broadcasters like NBC and CBS only granted "sustaining time" to religious programs sanctioned by the Federal Council of Churches. In theory and in practice this meant religious programming produced by predominantly East Coast, mainline Protestant churches. Less established churches, those that were predominantly evangelical and charismatic and some that were fundamentalist, were boxed out.

They had to pay their own way. Many started asking their viewers to support them

Asked about Wes long after Wes died, Don said that Wes had probably been sexually molested by one of the traveling tent preachers who visited Boone. It was more likely than not, Don said, but people didn't speak of those things back then. They talked about sin, and they talked about amazing grace. He was thankful that his unceremonious expulsion, this rejection from a father figure, hadn't alienated him from his faith forever. Merely for several years.

---

financially. Meanwhile, the Federal Council of Churches continued lobbying against the purchasing of airtime for religious broadcasting, claiming it would turn the Christian church into a beggar seeking handouts. Underneath their objection was a subtext not lost on many observers: believers so gauche as to have to ask for money to air their programs were low-class people.

Older mainline Protestant churches—the Episcopalians, the Presbyterians, the liberal churches—abandoned the airwaves. Those who remained had a more rural audience. Some evangelical programmers reacted by fulsomely congratulating their down-on-the-farm listeners. Charles Fuller of the *Old Fashioned Revival Hour* professed he was not interested in preaching to the citified or well-to-do.

On the contrary. "When I'm speaking over the radio, I'm not thinking of those in apartment houses or in the thriving cities, but my heart goes out to those who are up in the canyon creeks and the mining gulches and in the remote places." In every bitter cup God offers us, his wife and cohost, Grace, reminded listeners, there was a sweetness still.

These remainders also felt duty-bound to use new media as it emerged. "Television is the only way to reach the non-churched," Billy Graham argued in the fifties. "To say that the church shouldn't be involved with television is utter folly," Pat Robertson continued. Not to use new technologies would imply halfheartedness. The media was "the most formative force in America." The needs were the same, the message was the same, but the delivery could change.

MINNEAPOLIS

Rejection is hard to process when your worldview presumes that nothing just happens. You examine the results and have to consider two possibilities: Maybe you simply blew it. End of story. Or maybe it was blown—note the switch to passive voice—because you misapprehended God's plan. You thought you had heeded God's will, but you were wrong. You failed before you even started. Which is not comforting. Which is profoundly discomfiting if you believe nothing *just happens.*

In January 1987, a few months before our return to the United States, the televangelist Oral Roberts announced that God would call him home—by which he meant heaven—if his ministry did not receive $8 million in donations by March 31. He got the money.

✦

We unpacked our boxes with the televised Oliver North hearings on for background noise. Our new home was a two-bedroom apartment on the fringes of St. Paul in a new housing development built around old Northern Pacific Railway sheds. They had been refurbished to create Bandana Square, a venue for UNIQUE RESTAURANTS AND SHOPS, so a sign in the parking lot said. The sign was propped up high enough for cars speeding down Snelling Avenue to read. At the end of our street was a Days Inn.

In the hesitant light that came in through the sliding glass balcony doors, our family's failure to amass a decent record collection struck me suddenly as a huge error. First, there was the Amy Grant back catalog. A disco Handel's *Messiah*. Only two classical music albums: Mozart's *Eine Kleine Nachtmusik* and Mussorgsky's *Pictures at an Exhibition*. Then the original cast recordings of *Evita* and *Cats*. Diana Ross love songs. Amy's David Bowie and the 12-inch extended mix "Do They Know It's Christmas Time?" single.

Our problem is that our record collection is that of a homeless person, I thought. *If a homeless person with a shopping cart went foraging in dumpsters and Salvation Army stores, ours is the kind of record collection they'd arrive at.*

"I'm not even sure I believe in God," I whispered to another twelve-year-old at Camp Patmos one night after evening chapel, gesturing to convey that by "God" I meant all that surrounded us—the bowed heads and earnestness and s'mores, or that it only took a spark to get a fire going.

Danielle's eyebrows shot up. "What? What do you mean?"

"I mean," I said, gaining confidence, "sometimes I wonder if he exists."

Danielle slapped a mosquito that was threatening her thigh. "What are you going to do? Have you told your mom and dad?"

I wiped my runny nose on my new American jean jacket. I was going to do nothing. A person could think something for months and no one would notice. I was going to do nothing.

When we were summer visitors to the States, the rush of air-conditioning upon entering a shopping mall in June had felt like a kindness. Now it contributed to the sense that everyone in the country, from fellow shoppers to whoever it was that was in charge of the Muzak at Marshall's, was too interested in how you were feeling. Not because they really cared, but because they wanted permission not to have to think about you. Because if you were feeling good, and having fun, then they could safely ignore you. That's why everyone kept asking "How you doing today?" America wanted you to go to your room if you weren't doing so good, and not come out until you were ready for FUN. And if you weren't having fun, maybe there was something wrong with you, or maybe you didn't like fun, in which case there was definitely something wrong with you.

But anything could happen and that was exciting. Maybe we'd get rich now, I thought. Grandma Marian occasionally joined us on trips to the Rosedale mall, rubbing her arms to keep warm in the air-conditioning. She walked around with bemused smiles and when a sales lady asked her "How you doing today?" she'd say "Oh, wonderful, wonderful, thank you," and compliment the lady's outfit, even when the lady was wearing a shapeless smock identical to the smock every other Dayton's perfume counter lady wore. Marian flung compliments around the way small-town parade marshals threw candy, and didn't seem to notice or care whether anyone took her seriously. On the drive home from the mall she looked out her passenger side window and cluck-clucked at the disappearance of the elm trees that had once canopied the city's side streets.

"Dutch elm disease," she'd say, the way someone else might say "Pearl Harbor." As if Dutch elm disease were the most sobering fact she could conjure, a fate coughed into existence by Satan himself.

Did I know this poem, she asked, catching my eye in the sun visor mirror:

I think that I shall never see
A poem lovely as a tree.
. . .
Poems are made by fools like me,
But only God can make a tree.

Wasn't that nice? she asked. She had taught her students at the country school that poem. She was nineteen and had a whole bunch of farm kids to educate, grades 0–8 all in the same room, she said. Out loud I agreed it was a nice poem.

In the evenings we walked supermarket aisles and I felt pressure to be prettier, thinner, and lighter of heart. Dutch cereal had been muesli, Weetabix, corn flakes, porridges cooked on a stove. Here was an entire country of brightly colored, sugar-added, chocolate-added, are-you-having-fun-yet? At least in Holland you had *hagel slag*, the chocolate sprinkles strewn on neat tiles of white bread spread with just enough butter to make the sprinkles stick. You could eat this for breakfast occasionally and there was something nice and honest about it. *So, my child, you want sugar for breakfast? Here, have some chocolate and butter on white bread.* After that the kid owes the parent one. Breakfast wasn't some failed negotiation like Apple Jacks that pretended to promote healthy teeth and bones but fooled nobody, not even a sad mouth-breathing five-year-old. Maybe Apple Jacks was why American kids thoughts all adults were suckers.

✦

Mom took a job as an administrative assistant. No one said "secretary" anymore, but my mother didn't understand how her responsibilities were substantively different than a secretary's. She got the job after a few weeks of answering phones at the downtown St. Paul office of Northwestern Mutual Life Insurance. She'd been hired on the spot because she had a good phone voice and her name was Karen. *Northwestern Mutual Life, this is Karen* sounded correct. After a few weeks of observing her diligence, one of the senior agents—a real heavy hitter, a real go-getter, people around the office remarked— asked my mother if she would like to work for him exclusively. Dave already had a full-time assistant but would need additional help as his client pool aged and required more financial planning services. He also wanted to golf more. My mother was not interested in the insurance business but gratefully accepted his offer.

My father had a harder time finding work. He hoped to keep working in radio and thought his overseas experience coupled with on-air experience plus training experience made for a compelling résumé. He went knocking at Minnesota Public Radio. They disagreed that his résumé was compelling. He thought that perhaps KTIS, the Twin Cities Christian radio station, would be intrigued by his cross-cultural missionary experience. They gave him some gig work writing promos for *Sunday Night Live*, a new show that was to be like *A Prairie Home Companion* but evangelical. The show was not on the air for long.

Explaining the past nine years proved more difficult than he'd expected. His stories were met with blank looks. He got the sense that people resented him somehow, and that behind questioning hazel eyes was this thought: *So, Mr. Hustad, you got off the ride. Now you want back on. Please tell me why this should concern us?* A few weeks into this job search, Wes and Viv informed my parents that they were sorry to have to rescind their promise but they wouldn't be paying for Amy's college after all. They had come to the conclusion that it wasn't fair. *I see*, my father said, staring into his juice glass of Bailey's. *Not fair to whom?* The other grandkids, they said. *I see*, my father said.

The evening news aired special reports on "limits to growth" and how some Forrester Research analysts believed many Americans would have to adjust their expectations downward. But there was still the possibility, other talking heads argued, that the people worried about energy shortages had either (a) bought into an Arab conspiracy or (b) were Carteresque, cardigan-wearing nerds.

When burdened with a day's worth of warring thoughts, my father muttered and paced. He strode through the apartment, straightening piles of books, folding newspapers, collecting abandoned water glasses and depositing them in the dishwasher, pacing, muttering under his breath to himself and unknown third parties, practicing for hypothetical future conversations. The rhythms of his speech always matching his strides, a barked but discernable "Ha!" punctuating the air occasionally.

Someone gave us a blue Subaru clunker that gave off the appearance of food stamps.

One early morning in the first crisp chill of fall my father drove to a Christian businessmen's breakfast at the Radisson Hotel because he needed "contacts"—a new term to learn— and he didn't have any, not really, at least not the right kind. He parked the Subaru as far from the entrance as possible. Inside he met Andrew Lee, a Wharton School of Business alum and an executive at a global firm specializing in Human Performance Improvement. Andrew was unfulfilled by his professional success, however. He wanted to start his own company and call it PRISMA—Personal Renewal in Spirit, Mind, and Attitude.

"Don't think New Agey," Andrew told my father. He wanted to promote human development and self-actualization and though it wouldn't be expressly Christian in rhetoric, it was decidedly Christian in outlook in its emphasis on service to others. He had connections, Andrew told my father. He also had money. So did his family in Hong Kong.

"Are you interested?" he asked. My father was interested.

Business cards were printed and glass PRISMA logo paperweights ordered. But Andrew's contacts failed to materialize. My father proposed that they travel to China and hold workshops there on how to do business with Americans, and then, back stateside, in the conference rooms of Radissons and Marriotts and Ramada Inns, they conduct workshops for Americans on how to conduct business with the Chinese. The idea was perfect, my father said, his voice rising an octave with conviction. Andrew was fluent in Cantonese and Mandarin, correct? Andrew yawned at this suggestion. It was too crass. It lacked spiritual subtlety. He really just wanted to focus on fostering personal development in spirit, mind, and attitude. He also believed that my father owed him $10,000, but my father could not agree. The PRISMA paperweights disappeared from the home office tucked into the corner of my parents' bedroom.

Upon hearing that my father was back on the job market, the new pastor at Trinity Lutheran Church felt led to make some adjustments in the operating budget and give an unused office down the hall from his own to my father, who would have the newly created title of Missions Coordinator. When my father landed a second part-time job teaching speech to freshmen at a nearby Bible college, it seemed prudent to invest in an answering machine. My father recorded our outgoing message using the same DJ inflections he had used on TWR Bonaire. "Hello, you've reached the Hustads!" in the cadence of fast-running syrup and firecrackers. I asked if we could tone it down a little, because it wasn't as if calling and getting our answering machine was such a fantastic opportunity for people. Well, we didn't really know that, he said. Maybe it *was* a fantastic opportunity for people. *Don't discount the mystery*, he said.

Besides. We were very busy doing our best against a steady cadence of thuds. The garage door closing. The sound of worn Subaru tires in the snow: thud on 33 1/3 rpm. The sound of hip hitting the ice in the Target parking lot. Target! Once a place to buy shampoo, plastic picnic forks, and bags of charcoal; now, ballast in stormy weather.

The sound of a can of soup falling and rolling until stopped by the wheel of a shopping cart left obnoxiously, rudely, in arrogant defiance of all that was decent and warm and holy, outside the PLEASE RETURN YOUR CARTS HERE corral. My mother filled the dark-paneled pantry until each new item required the reshuffling of its contents so that more cans didn't fall, this time onto stockinged toes.

✦

Meanwhile, evangelicals were debating the morality and efficacy of church advertising. Some said it only made sense for them to be more aggressive as secular culture was getting so "in your face" and anatomically correct that the cultural pendulum had swung too far in their direction. Whereas in an earlier America there was pressure not to do certain things, now there was equal pressure to do them. Increasing the volume of Christian rhetoric was the only appropriate response.

Lack of interest in the church was a problem to be solved. Anyone would buy any product, the new church growth strategists said, provided it had the right promotional push behind it. Once you defined your target audience, the Holy Spirit would do the rest. Should a Christian college teach advertising techniques? This question was raised at evangelical conferences. Answer: of course it should. Beware of didactic expository preaching. Today's students required entertainment, razzle-dazzle, sound systems. If Christianity had any hopes of keeping pace with the seductions and allure of secular culture, old-fashioned exegetical preaching would have to go. Make Christian pencil cases and Christian bracelets and carve up the Bible and retranslate it to suit every conceivable market demographic—Bibles for teens, Bibles for women, Bibles for people who didn't like to read. Now something as simple as wearing a T-shirt could have a justified holy purpose. Spreading the good news was easy. Just put on a Christian T-shirt.

Here's how it works, someone explained to us: You wear the T-shirt that has, oh, I don't know, a Bible verse on it or something catchy, something that might lead a person to ask, "Hey what's that on your T-shirt?" At that point you were having a conversation, a real conversation, and you could tell this person how Jesus had changed your life.

"Cute idea," my father replied. He resolved not to put a Jesus fish on the back of the Subaru. If anyone asked why not, he said, he would simply say that sadly, our car had not accepted Jesus Christ as its savior. All this buying of trinkets to prove some affinity with God—it didn't make sense. And the megachurch flash and pop, surely men and women would leave the building thinking they'd worshipped when all they'd done was bathe in technologically advanced spectacle.

We had not encountered the word "stressed" in Europe or in the English books we'd read there. But here and now it was everywhere. Stressed? Take a bubble bath. Buy a Garfield the Cat spiral-bound desk calendar at one of Bandana Square's Unique Shops and feel more organized and thus less stressed. The Bible, too, some of the American Christians who'd stayed here, you know, the regular folk, they were saying that the life and work of Jesus Christ contained practical lessons on organization and leadership that could help one deal with stress. Read the four Gospels and get a picture of Jesus under a lot of pressure. Jesus experienced a lot of stress, they said. We could all learn from how Jesus dealt with stress. When the phone continued not ringing, my father would tell people we were "facing many challenges."

✦

I became a scholarship kid at a private Christian academy and learned that American twelve-year-olds were obsessed with perverts. It was another new word, and I learned it just in time because seventh grade teemed with suspected perverts. Kids worried that if they were caught wearing the same sweater twice in one week or picked their nose within sight of the captain of the boys' soccer team, they would become perverse. Perverted. On the bus ride home, an eighth-grade boy in black sunglasses, black jeans, and white T-shirt, same outfit every day, obviously embracing the pervert label, asked me and two other girls on the bus if we knew what was being suggested when he grabbed his crotch through his jeans. When he stared at us, tongue lolling to the side of his mouth, caressing his own nipples through his thin white T-shirt, did we understand what he was getting at?

We did. Seventh grade felt like missing a joke because you were down the hall in the bathroom, and when you walk back into the classroom, every face is aglow as the laughter fades. *What did I miss?* you want to know. You look from face to face but no one will tell you.

I picked up the paperback of *The Catcher in the Rye* that Amy had left behind when she went to college in Massachusetts—at Gordon, a small semiliberal Christian college that she hated at first—with passion—but the Freeds had recommended it and her Harvard application got bungled somehow. That the cover of *The Catcher in the Rye* did not feature a soulful young woman staring out a window onto sun-dappled trees seemed promising. Only the title and "J. D. Salinger" in yellow letters against a reddish-brown background.

"So my eleven-year-old daughter is reading *The Catcher in the Rye*," my father remarked when he halted by the living room sofa just long enough to catch the title before he entered the kitchen to open a jar of peanut butter.

"I'm twelve," I grunted. I smelled peanut butter and mayonnaise on white bread as he headed back upstairs to the master bedroom, where from the desk in the corner he made phone calls and continued looking for work. I kept reading until page 91, when the elevator operator asks Holden Caulfield if he's "innarested in some tail," and Holden asks, "Who do I pay?" Then I put the book down without dog-earing the page and stashed it in a cardboard box at the farthest reaches of my closet. Curiosity tugged on your sleeve but you could choose to ignore it, and I wasn't ready for this, this blatant non-Christianness.

I attended Wednesday night church youth group sessions because I was not prepared not to. I was initially expected to be better at God but everyone quickly realized that I was not. When the junior high youth group sat on the linoleum floor in a circle and clasped hands, eyes clenched shut against the hard overhead light, I could think of little else other than my desire to pray impressively, toggled with certainty that I couldn't. Popcorn prayers. Informal and unstructured, that was the idea. Just speak whenever you felt led to speak. I experienced this casualness as added pressure. Public prayers were a diving competition.

Sometimes I kept my eyes open so I could study the faces of those gifted with the ability to pray out loud, in public, as confidently as a pastor. The boys' foreheads unlined. The girls were more likely to moisten their lips during collect-their-thoughts pauses.

Lord, I just pray that we just . . .
I just ask you . . .

Every week we sang a song whose refrain was "We are in the world but not of this world." The idea that nonconformity could be claimed, not simply foisted upon you, sounded great. Another song was Micah 6:8 put to music:

He has shown you, O man,
What is good, and what the Lord requires of you
but to do justly,
and to love mercy,
and to walk humbly with thy God?

Another favorite song was lifted from Psalm 51, written by King David after he was confronted by the prophet Nathan. David's sins were plentiful: he saw Bathsheba bathing on a neighboring roof, seduced her, and upon discovering he'd impregnated her, arranged to have her husband—an officer in his army—sent to the front lines and certain death. David didn't murder the man but he might as well have. Verses 1–4 in the New International Version translation: *Have mercy on me, O God, according to your unfailing love, according to your great compassion, blot out my transgressions. Wash away all my iniquity and cleanse me from my sin. For I know my transgressions, and my sin is always before me. Against you, you only, have I sinned and done what is evil in your sight; so you are right in your verdict and justified when you judge.*

The King James version made for better song lyrics. We started in on verse 10: *Create in me a clean heart, O God, and renew a right spirit within me. Cast me not away from thy presence, O Lord; and take not thy Holy Spirit from me. Restore unto me the joy of thy salvation.*

We were absorbing the lesson that it helped to have a keen sense of our unworthiness. Sin was on a continuum, the youth group leader told us, and in effect God did not distinguish much between so-called big sins of adultery and murder and whatever smaller troubles we got up to—gossip and envy and putting on false fronts.

Philippians 1:21 came up a lot as well: *For to me to live is Christ and to die is gain.* Understanding this verse relied on a sophisticated understanding of the word "Christ." In the original Greek, we were told, "Christ" implied suffering on a spectrum somewhere between acute ache and chronic disappointment. The world we lived in was full of temptations and liars who promised us that compromising ourselves and our bodies would be harmless and consequenceless, but they were lying. They sought to separate us from God and then profit from our confusion and resulting pain.

But invite the Lord to enter into your heart, and a sense of internal organization would follow. Ask and it shall be given unto you, seek and ye shall find. How beautiful on the mountains are the feet of them who bring good news, who proclaim peace, who proclaim salvation, who say to Zion, "Your God reigns!"*

The youth group counselors lost me, however, when they asked us to imagine Jesus as friend. *Sure,* I thought. Surely Jesus wouldn't slop down some fake-nice sentences in my yearbook on the last day of school, bubbles dotting his *i*'s. Not only

---

*Matthew 7:7, Isaiah 52:7.

did saying, in one breath, that Jesus was God and in the next breath, that he was our pal, sound incorrect, it sounded desperate, as if just one sales pitch wouldn't close the deal. And in my view pals were like pets. Nice to have, but inevitably you'd move across the ocean and they would be put in a kennel and flown to Philadelphia and there eat table scraps out of some stranger's hand and forget about you. They were never *yours.* So why youth group leaders would want us to think of Jesus in terms of potential loss and jealousy mystified me. That feeling unworthy was a necessary precondition for experiencing God I could accept. Always. But Jesus as friend insulted us both.

Plus all these assurances that Jesus had experienced everything we had experienced or would ever experience. I mean, *gym class*, I whispered as I waited outside in the cold for my mother to pick me up, watching my breath form clouds, clapping mittened hands for warmth. *Hello.*

✦

The dining room in the house we moved to in South Minneapolis had "corner cabinets excellent for entertaining," according to the real estate agent's brochure, and that sold us on it because how dining room cabinets could possibly entertain was fun to contemplate. But my mother found it harder to create a sense of occasion now that overseas visitors weren't regularly flying in to stay at our house and inquire after native habits. We replaced the late-seventies carpet and resolved to remove the fake wood paneling in the back hall and basement as soon as we could afford to.

Our dining room table grew stacks of unfinished business. Notebooks and library books, bills and unanswered letters, place mats that should have been put down the laundry chute after yesterday's dinner but were not. When guests did stop by for French Silk pie and coffee, my mother told stories about our Holland experience that skipped the spreading-the-Gospel factor. Instead she talked about the fact that the Dutch, so tall and severe, were uptight about large household appliances. Unlike Americans, who did not modulate their enthusiasm for large household appliances. She spoke of being condescended to:

> So I go to the appliance store in Bussum—about a ten-minute drive from our house, and keep in mind there's no Sears or Kmart or anything like that—and I ask to see the clothes dryers. And the man—he's perfectly friendly—says to me, "Why do you want to see the dryers?"
>
> And I tell him, "Because I'd like to buy one!"
>
> [She pauses.]
>
> And then he says, very serious, "Do you own one currently?"
>
> "No, I don't," I say. "I have nothing. I'm renting, I mean. We're renting the house."
>
> Then he says, "So the owners did not feel it necessary to have a dryer?"
>
> [She pauses, grins.]
>
> "No," I say. I mean, what—? "No, apparently not!" I say. "But I would like one. I would like a clothes dryer."
>
> And then he asks how many children I have at home. Two, I tell him. And he says, "Only two children? So what do you need a clothes dryer for?"
>
> [The audience titters.]
>
> At this point I'm not really sure what to say, you know? Then he offers to show me some wooden drying racks and says, "Just put these in the same room as the boiler or hot water heater, you know, and you don't need a clothes dryer." So I try again: "I really want a dryer. I'm quite sure about this."
>
> "Wait," he says then. "Wait."
>
> "Excuse me?" I say, because this is not what I'm typically used to hearing from a salesman. "You should wait," he says. "Wait until you've lived in Holland for a while longer. Then you won't feel a clothes dryer is necessary anymore."

Story type two typically involved atheist expats. Enter Sheila Rolston-Horst, a wealthy wife of mixed English-Argentinian ancestry. Sheila had worked for Christie's auction house and my mother met her in the Van Gogh Museum cafeteria on her first excursion with the American Women's Club of Amsterdam ("founded in 1927 by four American women married to Dutch men" and with "a long tradition of helping American women feel at home in the Netherlands"). My mother had joined because she thought it might be nice to spend more time with people to whom you could say "I'll be thinking of you" and they wouldn't cringe because you hadn't said "I'll be praying for you."

Sheila introduced herself by glancing over at the croquette my mother was having for lunch and saying *Ugh, peasant food.* My mother replied that it was peasant food and delicious, and would Sheila like to try some? Within weeks Sheila was teaching my mother about wine, and my mother returned the favor by demonstrating how to shut off a washing machine one day when the maid was out sick and sudsy water was leaking onto the floor. You do not, my mother explained, have to yank the cord out from the wall the way you just did. Just turn this knob on the right here. (To us at home, that day, she mentioned the most important thing about Sheila: she had chosen the wine for Charles and Diana's wedding.)

These stories were met with polite titters, then conversation turned to the weather forecast.

My mother began canceling newspaper subscriptions and starting them up again. If the Minneapolis *Star-Tribune* began to bother her, we switched to the *St. Paul Pioneer Press*. Then vice versa. After work and a dinner of packaged tortellini with Prego sauce, my mother returned to the breakfast nook, a small TV in the corner tuned to *Entertainment Tonight*, and with the voices of John Tesh and Mary Hart two feet in the background, a small space heater humming, pored over articles left unread in her 7:00 a.m. rush of toast, jam, and black coffee.

The only parts of the paper she read in the morning were the front page and the obituaries. I wanted to know why the obituaries.

"I have to," she said. "I have to read them for work." It helped to know if a client had died before she got to the office and started fielding phone calls from grieving widows and the occasional hair-gelled son-in-law who had married for money. I knew it all depended—the toast and jam, the Prego sauce, the kitchen wallpaper—on her willingness to do this job she did not like. But I didn't know what to say. She would be changing into pajamas soon, and letting the end of the ten o'clock news be a signal that it was time to brush her teeth and get ready for bed.

Then she confessed that she had wanted to be a mortician.

"You're joking."

"No. I wanted to be a funeral director."

"You're joking."

"I'm not joking."

"That's gross."

"Well, your grandmother's cousin, Gordon Carlson, he owned the Carlson Funeral Home in Cambridge. You know them, you've been to their house. So I was used to being around the grieving process. And then I worked at a nursing home in high school. So I experienced a lot of sick and dying people there."

I continued protesting that funeral directing was weird.

"Your grandmother thought so. She said I'd have trouble finding a husband if I majored in mortuary science."

"She was probably right."

"Probably."

"So what did you major in instead?"

"Interior design."

"Ah."

"And then I—"

From the basement we heard the *MacNeil/Lehrer News-*

Hour theme music, the sound of the television clicking off, and my father's heavy slippered footsteps ascending the stairs.

"Then I dropped out after a year and married your father."

✦

She liked how he was so different. She was crowned a princess on the Cambridge High School Homecoming Court and he didn't talk much. He was the kind of boy who stood silent with his hands in his pockets, who said nothing when others might feel compelled to bring up the weather. He never leaned back in his chair to announce how stuffed he was from supper. He just said "Thank you."

She knew she was going to marry him three days after her brother Paul brought him home from Bethel College for the weekend so they could do laundry and eat pie. She made this announcement to Marian an hour after the boys left. Marian glanced up from stitching red cherries on a white dish towel. "You'll never marry anyone named Stanley." But the Tuesday of freshman semester finals week, he proposed. Dorm regulations at the University of Minnesota required she put on a skirt and sign out at the front desk before rushing out to meet him. The ring was no big thing. Sweet, appropriate. Wedding on August 6, 1966: ceremony at First Baptist Church of Cambridge jointly presided over by Orville and Wes. She sewed her own dress and veil, and the three fuchsia empire-waist bridesmaid dresses as well. Marian baked the white buttercream-frosted cake. Punch was nonalcoholic. A mixed marriage, men wearing plaid jackets and hearing aids yukked: a Swede and a half-Norwegian. She was nineteen, he was twenty-one, and they were photographed against the stuccoed hallway walls looking respectable, eager, and slightly stunned.

They agreed she would not be returning to the U. after the honeymoon. School was expensive, she had never really enjoyed it, and a $5,000-a-year starting salary teaching job awaited my father in Iowa. In Grand Junction she found work as a receptionist at a John Deere dealership. Other job responsibilities included filing invoices and wearing miniskirts.

✦

We rearranged the furniture often because exerting control over inanimate objects felt good. My mother typically announced her intentions midmeal. "I think I want to rearrange the living room," she'd say. Sometimes she wouldn't announce her intentions and we'd only learn of her restlessness by the sound of sofa dragged across carpet, the "Ow" of a stubbed toe. After dinner my father did the cleaning up. My mother cooked and he cleaned up—that was the deal struck. When this deal was mentioned it seemed pulled onto the stage as understudy for some other, unspoken bargain, like my mother agreeing not to be disappointed or my father having license to keep dreaming.

If my parents touched each other, I did not notice. We all stopped hugging. The bristles on my father's toothbrushes splayed dramatically to the sides within a couple of weeks of first use. *Wow, you're really brushing your teeth hard*, I'd remark. My mother didn't say much of anything one freezing October through the following March.

Amy came home for Christmas with instructions for making baked Brie. She had taken her knack for finding better things and applied it to new products and food and music; we had never eaten Brie in Holland. Amy introduced these items in the same voice our mother had used while guiding visitors through the Rijksmuseum. You would benefit from knowing about this, the tone gently said. Stopping at thrift/antique stores her eyes narrowed and I hesitated to interrupt her process of choosing. Beauty was at stake. Old porcelain saucers painted with African violets became receptacles for silver rings. Next to it, a cobblestone pried from a corner of Dam Square. In her eyes, everything wanted to form a tableau, and everything that could be taken out of context and given a new one would.

Her presence had a galvanizing effect in the house. Sharp new knowledge highlighted everything done wrong. The decorative throw pillows from Marshall's that had to be removed from the sofa before it could be sat on. The full pantry was also a problem. We stockpiled food as if expecting a *Little House on the Prairie* blizzard to trap us indoors for a week. We'd come far—obviously we didn't live in a house like the split-level rambler Wes and Viv occupied in Davenport, Iowa, with its brown shag carpeting, the television tuned to *Wheel of Fortune*, the bathroom vanities made of plywood and formica, the sofa sleepers bought at Levitz, the dust-gathering china because it was too nice to use. But still the people of New England owned bath towels that were not quite this color of Marshall's and making-do. Being envious was wrong and to arouse envy was wrong—so go easy on the pretty—but it was interesting to learn more about arenas where this ethos didn't seem to apply, and instead calm and excellence trailed you from room to room, matching the built-in bookcases.

I caught snatches of angry conversation. My dad's voice at his highest, most frustrated pitch. My mother's dropped low. Amy sounding officious as she restated her problem(s). She had again been prevented from registering for classes because the tuition bill hadn't been paid on time.

Isn't being in the States kinda like sitting in a wading pool? she asked me. *Like you're always scraping your butt on the bottom.* One night she reported that she made more money waitressing at a Massachusetts country club one summer than our father had scraped together our first year back in the States. Her conversation now held references to things like scallops and Camille Paglia. *When you're not here they argue about how they're going to pay for your plane ticket home and Visa bills and stuff,* I told her. Oh she'd always known, she said, she had always known we were poor. She mentioned how jokes about going around hat in hand, a sweaty-palmed family of four petitioning a basement full of churchgoers for monthly pledges, fell flat out east. Growing up a charity case wasn't a joke any-one knew how to laugh at, mainly because they didn't know what it was they were laughing at.

Into my stocking that Christmas Amy tucked a tiny green booklet. "I thought you'd like these," she said as I extracted the marbled green hardcover object from the jumble of black tights and ChapStick and Advil that our mother habitually stuffed in our stockings. Amy had filled the booklet with quotations—one per tiny right-hand page.

I knew that "I thought you'd like these" meant *I think you should like these* and I appreciated the guidance. She studied my face as I read:

> To be really great in little things, to be truly noble and heroic in the insipid details of every-day life, is a virtue so rare as to be worthy of canonization.   —Harriet Beecher Stowe

> The religious persecution of the ages has been done under what was claimed to be the command of God. I distrust those people who know so well what God wants them to do to their fellows, because it always coincides with their own desires.
>   —Susan B. Anthony

> I found God in myself and loved her fiercely.   —Ntozake Shange

> Adventure is worthwhile in itself.   —Amelia Earhart

> I have learned from experience that the greater part of our happi-ness or misery depends on our dispositions and not on our circumstances.   —Martha Washington

> He is still weak for whom his native land is sweet, But he is strong for whom every country is a fatherland, And he is perfect for whom the whole world is a place of exile.   —Hugh of St. Victor

To regret one's own experience is to arrest one's own development. To deny one's own experience is to put a lie into the lips of one's own life. It is no less than a denial of the soul.

—Oscar Wilde

I eventually placed the green marbled booklet on top of my dresser. Amy was either asking me to believe in women or dead writers. I was not sure which. But she obviously still loved me or otherwise she wouldn't care what I read, or how I turned out.

✦

There was always the possibility that the usual laws of thermodynamics could be suspended. Stuff rebounded, God willing.

My mother began drawing upon this idea after going to a Saturday morning garage sale with Marian and finding two blue pressed glass goblets. Not Waterford crystal, but nice. And what had happened, my mother remembered, was that some thirty years ago there was an afternoon gathering for church ladies at their house, and halfway through this buffet luncheon they hear a crash from inside the kitchen. Marian goes to investigate and there stands a scrawny girl with dirty arms and unbrushed hair, shards of blue goblet at her feet. My mother, eleven at the time—she couldn't really remember how old she was, but about the age when the sense of justice and ownership is most keen—was annoyed because all Marian said was "Oh my, let's get this cleaned up." Then she placed another blue goblet in the girl's hands. Within the hour this goblet was also in pieces on the linoleum. *Why*, my mother demanded to know once the last guest had backed her Oldsmobile out the driveway, was it okay for this girl to have broken *two* blue goblets? Why was Marian not angrier? And who did that smudgy little girl belong to, anyway?

Marian didn't answer those questions. "I'll get them back

someday," she said. Plus, they were just things. And so, garage sale, thirty years later, and my mother's looking through the box of 25¢ Harlequin romances and hears Marian clucking excitedly and goes over to investigate and Marian's holding two blue pressed glass goblets up to the light, one in each hand.

My parents decided that mailing $20 to a random recipient every week was the Christian response to their precarious financial situation and my father's persistent career worries. Their faith had faltered, but it was time to recommit, and a sure way to strengthen faith was to act on it. To live your faith when your faith made you nervous. Because the fear and trembling was where you stopped and grace began. So out went $20 each week because genuine Christians could not simply *say* they believed God would provide for them.

✦

I trusted no one to listen to my questions without rushing to answer.

Worship services on Sunday mornings became opportunities to gaze at the humiliations of middle age. The spreading stomachs, the slow shifting of weight from foot to foot as we stood to sing hymns. A few adults in the congregation were now lifting their hands into the air, palms to the sky, at select moments during the service. Such demonstrations were new to Trinity Lutheran and not universally admired. Some people in the congregation felt it was a little too showy.

The hand-raising's primary effect on me was to heighten my appreciation of the Apostles' Creed. Unemotional, almost mechanical in tone, it dropped the sanctuary's temperature—

> *I believe in God, the Father Almighty,*
> *maker of heaven and earth.*
> *And in Jesus Christ, His only Son, our Lord,*
> *who was conceived by the Holy Spirit,*
> *born of the virgin Mary,*

suffered under Pontius Pilate,
was crucified, died and was buried.
He descended into hell.
On the third day He rose again from the dead.
He ascended into heaven
and sits at the right hand of God the Father Almighty.
From thence He will come to judge the living and the dead.
I believe in the Holy Ghost,
the holy Christian Church,
the communion of saints,
the forgiveness of sins,
the resurrection of the body,
and the life everlasting. Amen.

—and fed a question: Was there a correlation between how matter-of-factly a belief was expressed and its sincerity?

✦

Sensing they had lost Amy, my parents tried a number of techniques to keep me interested in Christianity. They floated stories of their own rebellions like trial balloons. For example:

Did I know how short her miniskirts were when she worked at the John Deere dealership their first year of marriage? A skirt could not hang lower than the tips of your fingers when your arms extended flat against your side, my mother told me, and in the sixties this was as true for nice Christian girls as it was for anyone else.

Also! They used to get their cat drunk and they didn't go to church, either. *How did you get the cat drunk?* I asked. The expression on my father's face suggests he'd been wanting to discuss drunk cats for a long time. *You pour beer in his water dish.* Duh. Sam—that was the name. The black cat. Sam.

Oh, and occasionally they'd double date with Paul and his lady of the month. They'd pile into Paul's convertible and reenact the Kennedy assassination. Paul and Margie—or whatever her name was—in the back, Stan at the wheel, Karen riding shotgun. Stoplight changes, driving down Main Street, dazzling, white-toothed Paul and Margie waving at people on the sidewalk.

Then Paul clutches his chest, gasps, and slumps over into Margie's lap. Orville wasn't impressed but there was only threatened arrest for disorderly conduct when Paul—for some reason—refused to get his muffler fixed. Anyhow, preacher's kids. A special breed. Then Paul joined the navy and he looked really handsome in dress whites.

Then my father volunteers this: When he taught the Declaration of Independence, back at Rosemount High School, he had his white-bread suburban students read the Black Panther manifesto and DISCUSS. (Article 5: We want education for our people that exposes the true nature of this decadent American society.) I raise my eyebrows to signal an abbreviated *Thanks, Dad*, because it was truly a problem, to feel so contrary all by oneself.

✦

I was in the parking lot of Minnehaha Academy when I heard that the Rapture was coming—and that this was something to look forward to. The varsity tennis player Anna Qualin had been reading Frank E. Peretti's *This Present Darkness* and its sequel, *Piercing the Darkness*. Both excellent books, she said. Both super exciting and gripping. What was so interesting, she said, was that so much of biblical prophecy about the end-times and what it would feel like was actually happening right now.

Sure, I said.

Totally, she said. She squinted into the sun. It was early March and a bright sun was melting snow, glinting off the roofs of Jeep Cherokees. Of course the books were fiction, and a lot of the things that the book of Revelation talked about—wars in the Middle East, people turning away from God, and so on—had happened before. And yet there was plenty of reason to believe our time in history was exceptional. We possessed weapons that could wipe out the entire planet. We also had extensive communications and computer systems that would allow the Antichrist to gain control of the world easily. The people of Israel had returned to their homeland—check. The United Nations as one-world government—check.

On the appointed day, all faithful believers would be lifted to the skies and spared the torment that awaited everyone who had chosen not to believe in Jesus. Muslims, Hindus, Buddhists, atheists, Marxists, even some people who professed to be Christian but whose faith was lukewarm.

"You haven't read it?" she asked.

"Read what?"

"*This Present Darkness*."

I was reading *The Sun Also Rises*, but I didn't know how to say "I'm reading Ernest Hemingway" without causing someone concern.

"Nope. Haven't read it."

She smiled while adjusting the strings of her tennis racket. When she looked up she didn't look at me but over my shoulder to the melting snow dripping from a Jeep Cherokee passenger side wheel well. I got the sense that when she gave up her virginity, it would be reluctantly. I got the sense she'd grow up to be a gym teacher. Jealousy had gripped me when I gazed upon her type before, but now I saw a means of getting out ahead.

"Well, it's really exciting stuff," she said. "A very powerful message."

"Yeah," I said, gathering courage. "Doesn't it also say in the Bible that we shall not know the hour or the day? Something like that? Like, we're not supposed to care about when the world ends, or try to—"

She scowled as she bounced her racket off her right knee. I worried that I'd offended her. More surprising to me was the realization that I had meant to.

For a few months afterward I thought perhaps my problem

was that I was surrounded by the wrong kinds of Christians, and if I found better ones, I could hang on a little longer. A candidate emerged in Sophie Scholl, who was dead, unfortunately, but whose example inspired me. As students at the University of Munich, Sophie and her brother Hans wrote and distributed leaflets urging their fellow Germans to understand that Hitler's regime was contemptible, murderous, the war all but lost, and they ought to revolt. They were discovered, hauled in for questioning, and three days later sent to the guillotine. Their parents published their letters and diaries, all of which revealed Sophie to be an uncomfortable, itchy Christian, but an earnest one all the same.

"Whenever I pray, the words drain out of me," she wrote. "The only ones I can remember are 'Help me!' I can't offer up any other prayer for the simple reason that I'm still far too abject to be able to pray. So I pray to learn how to pray."

The book of their letters had a photo insert. They were young and not exactly beautiful but something stickier. I put a dime in the photocopier at the downtown Minneapolis public library so I could have a blurry black-and-white image of her looking down, hair short and windblown bangs like a *Sassy* magazine photo shoot. I cut along the borders and attached her picture to the inside of my locker door with blue poster putty. In the five-minute flurry between geometry and history, the hockey player whose locker was next to mine asked me if I was a lesbian.

✦

As my grandparents saw it, the problem—America's problem—had several roots. Too many people, and not just any people but prominent ones, the kind of people one read about in newspapers, had turned their faces away from God. Beyond that, the earthly rewards of rampant secularism seemed to be growing by the day. And too few people seemed to like the idea of making do anymore. So reminders of childhoods shaped by deprivation and pleasure in small things were kept on display, stored on shelves, where they could infuse the atmosphere with reminders to just eat whatever was on your plate and be fine with it. I picked up Marian's dust-jacketless hardcover of Vilhelm Moberg's *Unto a Good Land*, a Swedish emigrant novel translated into English and published by Simon and Schuster in the fifties. It was shelved next to a similarly ignored row of Reader's Digest Condensed Books, these, too, having faded into creaky family jokes. At what Baptist church fundraiser garage sale had they been purchased? Were they swapped for rhubarb pie? Did Marian only buy them because the seller had inoperable brain cancer, and a few extra dollars at a rummage sale helps people cope with impending death? Did you know Marian found 25¢ under the seat cushion of that scratchy horsehair couch, knocking the purchase price down to $1.50?

I wanted to know what exactly we were laughing at. Was our ability to congratulate ourselves on really minor accomplishments funny? Even more I wanted to know why Minnesota, of all possible and more interesting places?

The usual explanation was that Minnesota looked like Sweden, and so after landing at Ellis Island, our ancestors simply kept trudging until they saw the white pines, lakes, and granite that reminded them of home. This account had been confirmed by AARP members who had taken SAS package tours to Stockholm. Minnesota looked like Sweden—end of story.

Moberg's novel, however, begins on a boat quarantined in New York Harbor for three days as its human cargo awaits the all-clear from cholera inspectors. Inside the hold and pacing the deck are assorted farmers, youngest sons who would inherit nothing under Sweden's testamentary laws, religious dissidents, and Ulrika of Västergöhl, town prostitute. All had decided that life in their native country was intolerable and hoped that in America they could become different people, with different fates. And they ended up in Minnesota because someone knew some guy whose cousin had moved there eight, nine, ten years ago.

And because most every place else between the Hudson and Mississippi Rivers was already taken. Moberg's characters gaze out the portholes of the steamer that transports them across the Great Lakes and into the Midwest. Their children, when not gnawing on moldy husks of stale bread, whimper and cry— a good sign, because a child with the strength to cry is not dead. Wives squinted longingly at the pastures of Pennsylvania and Ohio. Were they there yet? America has no end! Would they be stopping soon? Need they traverse so many lakes and rivers to find a home? Couldn't they have found one nearer?

Nope! That's the answer they get. Sorry. They had to keep going until there was room, or until they reached that cousin, whatever his name was. Meanwhile they assured themselves that obtaining anything easily deprived a person of the purer joy of resourcefulness, the trembling in the fingertips when you are so tired yet so relieved.

From an attic stash of Orville's papers I knew that Orville's father, Johan Emil, had entered the United States at age twenty-two, and had traveled alone in steerage class with no luggage. "Just the shirt on his back and a bottle of vodka." According to the Cunard Line ticket, he'd paid $30.50 for passage from Göteborg to New York City on July 1, 1896. In 1900 he had his first portrait taken at a studio in Alden, Minnesota, though he now called himself John Emil. He sloughed off names like un-seasonably warm coats. His 1904 marriage license commemo-rates the union of J. Emil Johnson and Selma Lundin. They grew six children and potatoes. When the doctor said dry air would be better for Selma's asthma, they auctioned off the farm and tried Brownsville, Texas, and onions. Then back to Min-nesota, to a town called Fish Lake. This farm was more suc-cessful, though Selma didn't get to enjoy it for long, dying in her forties. Years go by, and Emil has less to say than ever. His grown children urge him to fly to Sweden to visit old relatives.

They could pool their money; it would not cost him a dime. But Emil shook his head. "I have no interest in doing that," he said. "No, no thank you."

On holidays we drove to Orville and Marian's house in Cambridge and to get there had to travel through a town called Blaine. Blaine's strip malls and Taco Johns and trailer parks made believing that God marshaled all human effort toward some greater beauty really hard to believe. Blaine was ugly like death from asphyxiation was ugly. Blaine made Amy, increasingly reluctant visitor to Minnesota, suck in her cheeks and hold her breath until her cheeks swelled up again, lending Blaine a *pffffft* sound effect as she exhaled through her mouth. Why did people build Blaine when they had to know, if only from books and photographs if they couldn't afford to travel, that we had other options?

When I was seventeen, Marian and I stood on the purple shag stairs of her Cambridge home and examined the jumble of new and old sepia-toned hand-tinted framed family photos hung in the staircase. Next to her wedding photo is a studio portrait of Orville's family, taken when he was college-aged. Orville, Hilmer, Mildred, Lillian, Irene, and Archie symmetrically arranged around Emil, whose wan smile is partially concealed by a mustache too prominent for sunken cheeks.

I asked Marian if Emil was tall, because he didn't look it. At 5'8" I cared. Tallness was important to me. She shook her head.

"Fairly short. Stunted I guess is what you'd call it. Life was hard there, back then. They didn't have a whole lot to eat growing up."

"But he wasn't, like, a midget?" I wanted reassurance that there were no short people in our bloodline.

"Like, five foot nine maybe. His kids all grew taller, is all I meant."

With that she returned to the kitchen to check on the pot roast, and I stayed staring at Emil's mustache for clues as to how he felt about having his strong-armed, corn-fed American children tower over him. Generations as a means to an end of transporting genetic material to a different place. Did that hurt at all?

Then Marian revealed that Johnson wasn't Emil's real last name. His last name upon boarding the boat that took him to the new world was Salomonson. By the time he exited Ellis Island, the last drop of vodka he'd ever drink several days behind him, he was a Johnson, and this was not the result of a clerical error made by a sleepy immigration officer, or so two pieces of anecdotal evidence suggested. One, he never sought to be known as Salomonson once he was established on his own Minnesota farm. Two, he never spoke of it. Johnson was no mistake; and considering that Sweden used a patronymic naming system at that time, and Salomonson quite literally meant son of a man named Salomon, we can assume Emil didn't much like his father, nor care to remember him.

In *Unto a Good Land* the Swedish peasants are still traveling by steamer and talking among themselves. Someone inquires as to whether they ought to report back to the family and friends left behind, which prompts Ulrika of Västergöhl to get loud:

"Write to Sweden?" she says. "But that country doesn't exist anymore! That hellhole is obliterated from the face of the earth!"

How so? She explains: The Lord God had long intended to destroy Sweden. But He had to wait until His people had left Sweden. As it had been about four months since their ship sailed, undoubtedly divine judgment had been meted out by now and Sweden had been erased from the planet.

So if any of these folks wanted to send letters home, Ulrika said, address them to Hell Below, assuming mail was delivered there.

What now bothered me about evangelical talk of salvation: It didn't involve sufficient risk. It conflated coziness with innocence, and I wanted neither. I decided that God, if he existed, preferred sins of commission. He must. How could he not? Sins born of big appetites were more interesting to watch than sins of omission—those things we did not do that we should have. It was tedious to watch someone not care enough, or pretend not to notice someone hurting because to have noticed, truly noticed, might mean we'd have to break our routine and help.

At night, alone, I hastily reordered my rankings of sins. Fornication and cursing—surely these were minor transgressions. Cowardice and complacency? Far more despicable.

✦

Tips for the girl who loses her virginity when losing her virginity signifies a rupture with years of Wednesday night youth group preaching on how to be:

- Work up to it.
- Wait until the week you turn eighteen.
- Do it with a long-haired boy who won't be alarmed when afterward you cry chest-heaving sobs, as if your body hadn't been entered but fear was attempting to leave it. Let him spoon you. Whisper. Don't use a Kleenex but let tears and snot tell the pillowcase.

✦

First I tried black hair, then red. My mother and I argued for a week about serving meat at my graduation open house. *I don't want it*, I said. *People expect it*, she said, especially older people like Lois Olson from Trinity for whom vegetarianism is a new and threatening idea. The fact that our former TWR supporters bearing $10 checks tucked inside Bible-versed Hallmark cards would be coming to my graduation open house didn't obligate us to design the menu around them, I argued. But vegetarian might make people uncomfortable, she said. My mother won that battle but lost me.

I sought the company of other young men and women who didn't shop at vintage stores but at thrift stores, and the difference, I could explain, was not just money but between people who wanted things selected for them and neatly ironed and dry-cleaned before purchase and those who wanted to find their own treasures, those who could see possibility where others saw filth and germs. I wanted to be around people who truly understood how the American sociopolitical order was stapled together, which was—if you had to ask—terribly. If this country had come off the copier at Kinko's, you wouldn't even bring it up to the counter to pay for it. You'd let it fall into the recycling bin and pretend it never happened.

College brought more angry young people who thought settling for one's natural hair color was weak, that President Bush had been a bloodless blue-blood disaster and President Clinton was hardly an improvement. They thought I could be more casual about sex; it wasn't the combining of souls. It was, in fact, like sneezing, and why did I still think of "soul" in reference to anything beyond a particular type of music, anyway?

I also encountered my first Americans who associated religious belief with rank stupidity. Plenty of unbelievers in Holland, sure, but there churchgoing was still seen as a legitimate pastime. It was assumed that people who believed in God at least knew what they were doing. This was not the case here. I embarrassed myself in my American Identities class when—upon hearing the term "Protestant work ethic" for the first time—I tentatively protested that getting up at 6:00 a.m. wasn't, you know, a Christian thing per se. Megan, a classmate, sighed. *It's a concept; it's been around for a while.* I switched schools because I thought the problem was venue, not my restlessness. There I met more alienated youth. We knew how to fold a half square of toilet paper so that it remained lodged in the ear canal. Standing four feet in front of a guitar amp in a crowded basement while a four-piece punk band played was hard on the ears, and we didn't want to damage our hearing too much. We wanted to damage our hearing a little. One could buy foam earplugs, but then again you could also decorate your home with brand-new sofa sleepers from Ethan Allen, or watch *Full House*, or buy Pearl Jam CDs from Sam Goody. All these things were technically possible but not things a thinking person did. I met my first true hippie, a nice guy in tie-dye with thick light brown curls that hung to his shoulders. "I'm good," he'd say. As in, "No, thank you, I don't need another hit off that joint," or, "Oof, thanks, no more ice cream." I was amazed by this. I had never heard it before. "I'm good." Who could say such a thing about himself? He felt good and felt he was good. Impressive. All these people, so pleased with where life and their convictions had taken them, hippies and the young evangelicals in their WWJD gear alike. What Would Jesus Do? Hard to say, I muttered. Dunno. Maybe tell you to take off that stupid bracelet and shut up?

My father and I got into a big argument after he made a comment, apropos of Minneapolis's "ghetto in the sky," as everyone called it, a public housing development not far from the University of Minnesota and the banks of the Mississippi, that it was a bad idea to concentrate the poor like that. "It encourages pathologies," he said. I had been reading *The Nation* and told him that was offensive. Poverty wasn't a crime, I said. Warehousing people, he said, that was the problem. As soon as you achieved such a high concentration of poor people, creating an environment in which they're only surrounded by other poor people, only looking at other poor people, only hearing other poor people talk, then you have problems.

I had recently absorbed the fact that scholars had studied the pathologies of people like us. According to their theories my parents placed a premium on good behavior because indulging appetites could land us in trailer parks. More comfortably situated aka rich people saw the poor as impossibly other, whereas the asset-poor middle class looked at people in the welfare lines and saw themselves—minus the ability to keep their pants on, delay gratification, or stop smoking. Poverty was just one or two bad decisions away. So the Christ-minded middle-American middle class fixated on sins that historically had increased one's chances of sliding down the economic ladder (abortion being the one notable exception). How nice for you, I now thought to myself, that being a good Christian lines up so well with everything you do anyhow as reliable employees.

At Wes's funeral Viv surprised everyone by placing her hand on the casket and telling him that he'd been a wonderful husband but a poor father. My father related this matter-of-factly, hints of grim vindication moistening his eyes. He barked a laugh. Ha! It was really funny, when you thought about it, he said. It's not like Vivian had ever displayed this knack for dramatic timing before.

My father and I were in the car again. It was a newer car, because the Subaru had been given to a Liberian exchange student named Flomo Bucket, who via some informal Christian network had ended up a boarder at Orville and Marian's house and was taking accounting classes at Cambridge Community College because his entire family had died in the civil war.

We are feeling oppressed because the Minneapolis sky takes on a half-lidded quality on overcast days in December, as if more reluctant to face time than you are. But the cold let you fiddle with the defroster and vents instead of talk. I concentrated on the windshield.

"I really don't like winter," my father finally said.

"I don't either," I said.

He asked what would be keeping me busy this semester. The usual, I said. Study, job.

"You won't agree on this," he said. "But one of the things I know for certain is that a completely secular outlook is not enough."

I concentrated on the dashboard. If I said nothing, we could make it to our destination without getting into an argument. I thought of my boyfriend and how, so he'd told me, his mother in her twenties had casually shrugged off her Christian Scientist upbringing, let it drop like a shawl as she swanned into cafés, filled her own house with watercolors, seashells, a tall husband, books, and kisses, and sent her two handsome sons off to art schools in interesting cities. *Secular outlooks seem to work just fine for some*, I thought.

Instead I asked:

"What do you mean, exactly?"

"I mean that if you haven't developed a spiritual understanding, you will not be fulfilled. If you're living a purely secular life, you won't . . . You'll be missing a layer."

I remarked that it seemed to me that the evangelical habit of saying "I feel led" was just Midwestern self-effacement. Because in this mindset, you couldn't simply say, "Here's what I'm going to do." You had to blame somebody else. You could never just take a job in Cincinnati. You had to say, "I feel God is calling me to Cincinnati." And wasn't it convenient that after these people announced that they were putting these decisions in God's hands, God usually just told them to do whatever they secretly intended to do all along? Were they so insecure that they needed God's backup for every tiny decision they made? They hauled God into the story because they were fearful of their own power to create or destroy.

"I wouldn't disagree," my father said.

Then we halted the conversation because we didn't want to push our luck.

I told people I wanted to move someplace where I wouldn't have to deal with such harsh winters. *Oh, the cold builds character*, some responded. *I think I have enough character*, I'd say. *More might be overkill.* That was my way of making sure everyone understood that I wasn't interested in doing or saying what the situation required. A great aunt—Arlene, reliably sobering—stared at my insolence and dark lipstick and put down her pie fork and said *But winter is winter anywhere you go*. And I looked at her and thought, *No, you silly woman, no it is not*, and for years afterward I assumed we'd both been talking about climate but now it dawns on me that we weren't.

When a boyfriend and I packed a Ryder truck to move to New York, however, I hadn't figured this out yet. All I wanted was space for unruly opinions. I was grateful, in a small, stingy way, for parents who at least understood that lives were made in leaving. What did Adam and Eve do, after they ate the fruit from the Tree of the Knowledge? They left the Garden of Eden. Granted, that decision wasn't their own—

My parents wished us traveling mercies. They prayed I wouldn't wind up with a syringe in my arm, bleeding in sinful gutters. They handed me an envelope containing $400 in cash. They gave until it pinched and gave more. When a ball of warm bread and saliva hits your stomach and soaks up the fear and acid, relief ripples cell to cell. Immediately. Unmistakably. But maybe it was an error to imagine that an end to bigger hungers felt similar. Perhaps it wasn't pleasurable at all.

NEW YORK

p. 76. What does it really mean "to be alive"? This involves a certain quality of intellectual life which we will be studying in the next chapter. Above all to be alive means the total situation of man as he is confronted by God; this is precisely what our world wants to forget, and wants to make us forget. It does this in many ways: in its philosophies and in its thought, as, for instance, in materialism, spiritualism, surrealism, existentialism, essentialism; as well as in concrete action, of which we have already said enough. In all spheres of human life, there is an immense effort to prevent man from entering this total situation where he is alive.

—*The Presence of the Kingdom*

+

My people never found groups we wanted to remain in. After twelve years my father stopped wanting to be known as a schoolteacher. He was a missionary for nine years only. He never worked for a company.

Great-great-grandfather Paul Hustad saying to hell with the entire town and starting his own church on the edge of his farm. Young Clara refusing remarriage. High-cheekboned Emil at the head of the Sunday table, wordlessly chewing stainless steel forkfuls of mashed potato, refusing his children's notions of where home was.

We had a knack for sullen independence. This sullen independence got us to the margins, and we felt most alive there. Wherever we belonged, we wanted out. Once comfortably seated with a white cloth napkin across the lap and the waitress walking over with a glass of water, no ice, we looked around the dining room and started thinking about change. Changing the light fixtures, the company, or our company's mind. We liked changed minds.

We were dreamers but not easily impressed. This is an enraging combination. It insists on its own accounting system, and the columns never align.

✦

The first thing I lost upon moving to New York was respect for the concept of deserving. "You deserve it," people said. They said it to each other, often in the context of job promotions, sometimes in reference to a particularly nice boyfriend. It sounded like the *You've come a long way, baby* Virginia Slims cigarette advertising spreads I studied in my mother's sea breeze–damp copies of *Good Housekeeping.*

But before the idea of deserving made me cringe it was gorgeous, because when you move to New York City everything feels like a reward. You're rewarded for imagining you might survive the uprooting. You're rewarded for asking the questions that get answered here. For realizing that by coming here you've agreed to a proposition: that the size and scale of the competition will either cause you to abandon the ambitions you packed, or redouble your commitment.

This new arrival mania animates every sidewalk. The streetlights glow with you in mind. You step out of one of the last dive bars on Houston Street and walk to the corner of Mulberry Street and glance north and the Chrysler Building is still there, it hasn't moved since you last checked, and it's beautiful. This is your reward for paying attention. The WALK sign turns green as you approach, and this is your reward for being a pedestrian. Strangers risk humiliation to discover what you smell like. This is because you've fooled them into thinking you're more attractive than you actually are, and the reward for that skill is attention, which in turn leads to free food and drink, which is handy because your salary is modest.

I admired the courage of every come-on. The ones I refused I turned down gently because I felt we had something in common, these men with no chance and I. That I had a job at Random House was a fluke. I'd scanned pages and pages of job listings in the Sunday *New York Times*. I didn't have a computer so I walked to the Kinko's on a Brooklyn street called Manhattan Avenue with a floppy disk containing my résumé and typed up a cover letter on a machine rented by the quarter hour. I asked the Polish counter girl how much extra to send a two-page fax to a 212 number. I kept the receipt for $12.40 because the paper was pistachio green and register ink gray, and I feared I might forget what it felt like, this waiting for my existence to make sense, and this receipt would ensure that I didn't.

Once I got the job, I started receiving compliments. "You don't seem Midwestern at all" was one, or at least I accepted it as such because that's how it was intended. They meant *You're not doughy*. But mostly they meant *You seem like one of us*, and while I could not agree sober, I did after the second drink.

I grinned when someone commented on how little protection I had against the elements. They were usually referencing the fact that I was out on the fire escape smoking in forty-degree weather in just a sleeveless blouse, my coat and manuscript bag bundled and thrown into a dark corner inside. But I liked to imagine they were referencing the fact that I was miles from anybody required by blood or custom to love me, and had so little experience talking among the smart set. On weekday mornings, when deli cashiers called me "sweetie," I felt grateful and recognized. Maybe if I were sweet I would survive, and if I could be certain I'd survive, the emails I exchanged with friends wouldn't have to be clever. *Dear Megzo: Sorry I didn't return your call. Was in Thailand. Am back now. Let's party* and *The suit says yes, but the red lipstick says no* and *Here I damply sit, correcting page references for the index of a Noam Chomsky reissue. But it was lovely to run into you last night* and *ANY-WAY, if you find you need something, maybe like actual chicken soup as made by a Jew, very potent, let me know* and *I think I engaged her in a too-long conversation about Winnipeg* and *Mine was a blue-gray, turned-up collar, Neil Young–listening, trudging-through-dead-leaves, back-and-forth-to-the-studio kind of weekend* and *An unidentified fellow waiting for the bath-room said, "Hey, you're that girl who was smoking"* and *I am good. An animal. Enviable. Chilly (no heat in my office). How are you?* Every email was confirmation that cities were the perfect hiding place. Someone pointed out the obvious: cities have a bad rap with Christians because they daily let us prove that the human heart's true desire is to look at one another, not up.

Thoughts of a pre–New York past hit me glancingly and in-stantly dispersed. A suitor would remark on my peculiar accent, or my un-American teeth. *Yeah, well,* I'd say, *when I was at the age most Americans get braces, the Hustad family had other con-cerns.* Then I'd grin, so he'd know religion and I were old pals but it was all water under the bridge. I became adept at chang-ing the subject. *You sound like Stewart Copeland,* a middle-aged man once told me. *Who's that?* I asked. *The drummer for the Police,* he said. *Oh yes of course,* I said. *Yeah, you've got sort of a pan-Atlantic thing going on,* he added. And so I trot-ted out that story every subsequent time my voice came up— let's not talk about missionaries, this meant, let's talk about middle-aged men and their lingering love for eighties rock bands.

I snatched and stored as many compliments as I could be-cause I worried. I worried that I wasn't doing a good enough job. I worried that when I gave compliments to other people, I had concentrated on the wrong virtues and congratulated people for their knack for making do when I ought to be admiring their winner's instincts. Walking to work in the morning, the same self-chiding voice: *Be careful or you'll lose everything. Great posture but you should really stop catching your reflection in store windows so often.* I protest weakly that I'm not looking at me so much as me in this world, to remind myself that I'm in it. *Bullshit,* my other self replies. *You're just vain. God doesn't like that.*

To my mother I described the sensation of striding up to the Random House offices at 299 Park Avenue as being "like something out of a movie" because she would like that idea and because it was true. Park Avenue just north of Grand Central Terminal is four lanes of yellow-cab traffic honking in each direction, St. Bartholemew's dome plus the Seagram Building and the fountain where Audrey Hepburn whispered to George Peppard about breakfast at Tiffany's or his future on *The A-Team.* Next door was the Waldorf-Astoria Hotel and when the U.N. Security Council met, every Random House employee had to walk blocks out of their way because the streets would be closed to all traffic, but this, too, was a reward, a reward for being where everyone wanted to be.

Three floors up, an atmosphere of hesitation permeated the office, a worry that the combined forces of a public no longer enamored of books and a parent company demanding 15 percent annual growth would force layoffs. *Back in the day,* you'd hear a senior staffer say, *back when William Faulkner dropped by the office, a person might return from lunch to tiptoe past Mr. Faulkner snoring on the reception area settee. Back then people had more time and larger offices with windows that opened.*

It was like walking into a party and being told, if only you had been here an hour ago. But right now seemed magical enough to me. I invested in preppy clothes because I figured if we were going to pretend it was the early sixties, I should look the part. Opening the first shipment of any book felt sacramental. The box was always too heavy to lift so I slid it down the carpet from the maildrop to the place we wanted to be when its contents saw daylight, which was never in the privacy of an office but out in the hallway, in view of witnesses. I was careful with the X-Acto knife so as not to slice the unlucky books on top. A slight hush preceded the moment we lifted out the first book. One day I passed the freebie bookcase where excess books were stored until someone claimed them. Some were hardcovers that had since been made into paperbacks, some paperbacks we happened to have in greater quantities than we had readers, and they remained there for months. *Books we can't even give away*, we grimaced when visitors pointed. Dinged-up books also found their way to the freebie shelves, which is how I discovered my employer had published *The Technological Society* and *Propaganda* in mass market paperback editions. I brought them home and read only as far as the publisher's note at the beginning of *The Technological Society*. The gist: The editing and translation had taken so long, and sucked up so many company resources, that they began referring to it as "Knopf's folly," but they persisted because Aldous Huxley said it "made the case" he had attempted to make in *Brave New World*. That love of efficiencies spread like algae. That "previous societies took their character to a very large degree from the men in them" but ours was shaped more by our techniques and test scores and machines. I closed the book and got on with being forgetful.

After work the assistants went out for drinks lugging manuscripts in shoulder bags. It was eight o'clock by the time we ordered our first round. No one expected us home and we were beholden to no person or cause until the next daybreak and we took this freedom seriously. We felt obligated to turn the day's work upside down. I waited tipsy on subway platforms that returned me to Brooklyn via Queens, and some evenings I

New York sublet on the corner of Houston and Lafayette and a lucrative job at a consulting firm. He advised Seagram's CEO, Edgar Bronfman, Jr., on how to sell more cognac to racial minorities. How did his interdisciplinary degree with a concentration in art history qualify him for this work? his friends teased, though everyone knew the answer. He was handsome and 6'1" and spoke from a low register. When the work began to bore him, he quit to travel around India. He bartended at a French restaurant for a few months. He liked the regulars, the methods, the instant gratification of wiping down the surface of a decades-old bar top. Then he was off again to obtain his MBA in France and drive around the countryside in a borrowed 1965 Mercedes. He returned to New York again to cofound a technology company. Figures like $39 million were thrown about by a much larger company interested in acquiring it. That figure was tossed about as we tore off handfuls of semolina bread and smeared them with jam, the Sunday *Times* for a place mat. His apartment was high-ceilinged and sparsely furnished. It had beat-up wood floors. Above the cupboards in the kitchen he'd arranged a row of Café Bustelo coffee cans.

We had met at a second-floor bar on Canal Street everyone called "the Bulgarian bar." My friends and I had just been to the Film Forum. We were ordering our first round. He tapped me on the shoulder. "We've met," he said. "No, we haven't," I said, which though factually accurate might have served as a warning to him of my drive to disagree.

He was correct in that we had been in the same room before, at a Christmas party held at the Thirteenth Street loft of a well-known novelist. I had crashed with some other assistants. It was a Wednesday night and we came straight from work. Monica Lewinsky was there. James had escorted a female friend who dissuaded him from approaching me because it was too soon after his last relationship. It was mid-December and we didn't know who the next U.S. president would be. I kept catching his glance but talked to a legal analyst for NBC News who was covering the 2000 election recount. Partygoers kept stopping to congratulate him on his reporting. He deserved his newfound success. I stood in line for the bathroom and when the door opened to let in the woman standing in front of me, a trim dark-haired Italian woman in her forties, she turned and grabbed my hand and told me I'd be joining her. *Men like a little mystery*, she explained. *So. Never go to the bathroom alone.* I half expected her to start cutting lines of cocaine once the door shut behind us but instead she started smoothing her hair. *Duh*, I scolded myself. She was not carrying a purse and her tight black pants were pocketless, her arms bare, and there was not, as someone at the office had told me to expect, a mirrorful of cocaine amid the votive candles flickering on top of the toilet tank. I pulled up my skirt and sat down. She stared at herself and ran quick fingers through her hair as I peed. She reapplied red lipstick. We switched places. *You're wearing a turtleneck*, I scolded myself again. *A yellow wool turtleneck. How about next holiday season, when getting dressed in the morning, you remember there are parties like this, and you don't put on the yellow wool turtleneck.* The Italian woman and I exited the bathroom to raised eyebrows.

James and I had dinner three weeks after the Bulgarian Bar meeting at a small Dutch restaurant on Thompson Street. We did not say the obvious, which is that it was great good luck that we had been given a second chance, that he now had the opportunity to tell me why he had worn a burgundy velvet smoking jacket to that Christmas party. When a man's evening is assured to be absurd, he said, because "Christmas" and "hosted by the author of *American Psycho*" should not be in the same sentence, he pulls out the mothballed burgundy velvet smoking jacket, the jacket his grandfather Sammy gave him, the one with too-short sleeves. I thought I had cracked a code.

But I still did not understand why saying someone was deserving was seen as such a nice thing to say. Taken to its logical conclusion, it implied that some other people were not deserving, and I worried about those people. I worried my family fell in that category. I worried I fell into that category.

That worry burbled out in moments when I had my head tilted back on the arm of James's large white couch and was reading a manuscript, limbs splayed in every direction, and he'd announce that he would like to paint. I lowered the manuscript pages to my chest so I could see him smoking Marlboro Reds by the window.

"You what?"

"I'd like to make art."

"Art?"

"Art."

"What do you mean?"

Well, he said, he liked painting and he knew some people who had started out small, showing their work in galleries owned by friends, maybe not in New York but definitely in Toronto, and it was by no means an immediate living but it was feasible. I choked on my indignation. Out of my mouth came a passionate dissertation on Erik, an ex-boyfriend, who had grown up white trash in central Minnesota in a shitty small town and moved out of his parents' house at sixteen because he won a scholarship to an arts high school in the city, and got his own apartment at age seventeen, an apartment in a neighborhood so bad that one day he stepped over a dead man to get to his front door, and all throughout he worked night shifts in restaurants, starting as a dishwasher and maneuvering his way up through prep and fry stations then at last a sous chef job, collecting burn scars on his forearms to jostle the paint splotches, and not to mention the year he couldn't afford a studio, when he—when we—slept in the same room with the turpentine fumes, mangled cheap Chinese brushes soaking in his kitchen sink. And how now Erik was cooking in Brooklyn restaurants until 1:00 a.m. in T-shirts worn so thin you could trace his rib cage through them, all for afternoon sun to paint by and decent canvas. And now James wanted to scooch his Master of the

Universeness aside and pick up art, as if all options were open to him.

It was important to me that the sun not set before I had convinced James that what he wanted was absolutely not possible and he was stupid for even considering it. I thought this was the right thing to do. I thought I was helping him, and New York, and Harvard, be more realistic.

In the week following September 11, 2001, we stared at each other over vodka and sodas and an ashtray. The evening of the thirteenth, with CNN blaring in the background, he said he felt as if there was no point in continuing with anything. I told him he was being silly. Then, months later, because I didn't know how to say "I do love and admire you" and I could not say "I am scared and want someone to take care of me," I stood at my kitchen window in my Brooklyn apartment, sipping a vodka and soda and staring at the end of my Marlboro Light, then at the anxious dog tethered to a too-short chain in the neighbor's yard below, and said into the phone that our paths had been so different and I didn't think he could ever understand me so it would probably never work out between us and I said all this in hope that he would try to convince me otherwise.

"Megan," he kept saying. "I just want you to be happy."

This I took to mean I wasn't good enough as I was.

When James broke up with me for the third and last time, I begged for understanding. He said no, he was done. I cried in the office bathroom and off and on for three years, mostly because I couldn't blame him.

"He was an asshole," friends said. "Maybe," I said. "But that's kinda not the point."

A couple of years later, in a briefly sophisticated attempt to be friends, we spoke on the phone again. He informed me he was dating someone new. Anka. She grew up in Moscow and worked in fashion.

I asked James what he was looking for.

Silence.

"In a partner," I clarified.

"Someone like you," he said. "But with more self-awareness and more self-control."

✦

How to talk about missionaries when talking to people who hate the idea:

- Joke. ("Yes, an anachronistic career choice, I know." And: "Missionaries in Holland, yes. Roughly a thousand years after the first ones. Seems a little late to the party.")
- Use "itinerant" when describing the evangelists who came to Intracare to study. Not everyone knows what "itinerant" means. Often they will be embarrassed by not knowing and won't ask for clarification. Also, while it is acceptable to express impatience with American Christians, the etiquette concerning Ghanaian Christians is less obvious.
- No one challenges the basic wisdom of sparing the people of Ghana a visit from missionaries from Grand Rapids, Michigan, and replacing them with homegrown itinerant evangelists.
- Mention your mother's surprising equanimity on the subject of prostitution.
- Mention the desire for stamps in passports. The person may nod—stamps in passports, more of them. Of course. Very desirable. Smiles all around.

✦

"I wish we knew how to ski," Amy says. "I wish Mom and Dad had taken us skiing when we were young."

"Why?" I don't understand.

"It's something people know how to do."

"Yeah, but not everyone," I say. "Like us, for instance. We don't know how to ski. Besides, I'd plow right into a tree if I went skiing."

"But if we had learned when we were younger . . . Maybe.

We lived in Europe, after all. It wouldn't have been all that difficult or that expensive to go to Switzerland. Our classmates went on ski vacations every year, and not just the rich kids. It really wasn't a big deal."

The main reason I was unwilling to accept this line of reasoning was I had zero interest in skiing.

"Sure, but Mom and Dad weren't into skiing. They weren't into sports of any kind. We're a physically uncoordinated people."

"Still," Amy concluded. "It would have been good for us to learn how to ski."

Amy was living in Boston—no, Cambridge, in a duplex apartment not far from Central Square—when she said this. She had a roommate and a shelter cat that she had named Shouty Crackers. Above her bed was a beautifully framed print of a line from T. S. Eliot's *Four Quartets*. An artist boyfriend had made it for her. She no longer had the boyfriend, but evidence of his affections still enjoyed prime placement in her decorating scheme.

"Maybe you'd like it better in New York," I say, because I took her to be saying that she had a hard time copping to her missionary upbringing in the People's Republic of Cambridge.

She bats that idea away. Something about Cambridge appealed to her instinct for competition. If there was turf she wanted to win in, Cambridge, Massachusetts, was it. Still she felt handicapped by memories that not only failed to impress but raised eyebrows. Instead of ski lessons we had been trained to seek charity, our grubby paws out not unlike the gypsy children in Paris schooled in panhandling.

"But you've had such amazing jobs since college," I press. "You've traveled the Silk Road, you've been to Hong Kong, Pakistan, Tibet, Thailand, Vietnam, Kazakhstan. In Vietnam you and that Berkeley professor with the mustache . . ."

She sighs the sigh of a woman tired of having to explain herself. "It's not, it's not—"

Meanwhile my father's business hadn't achieved liftoff. He had set himself up as a life coach / speaker / writer and seller of books that would help individuals in the financial services and related industries market themselves better. His rhetoric wasn't explicitly Christian but he drew on Christian themes, and the company name—Press Toward the Mark—was taken from Saint Paul's letter to the church at Philippi, King James Version.* His clients appreciated the spiritual angles to my father's delivery. Talking to him, they felt larger somehow. He talked to them of "Free Agent Nation," an article he read in *Fast Company* and found really inspiring. Checks arrived sporadically, and there was the constant hustle. But he was adamant that he would not be returning to teaching. One, the public school system sucked. Two, because he wanted to be part of the 3 percent—he had read extensively on the subject—who had written down goals and achieved them. Returning to his past was not on his list.

So we press on, he said. He was grateful, he said. Echoes of talk radio crept into his speech patterns—the cadences of men frustrated that this world has not recognized their full value. Thoughts on current events he prefaced with "People forget." On the unintended consequences of feminism and the expansion of professional opportunities for women: "People forget that women only had two career choices: nursing and education," and he dropped into a reminiscence on the great teachers he had at the Marshalltown, Iowa, community college. His point was that women's access to a broader range of careers had resulted in a brain drain in some fields.

I didn't like how "People forget" implied that life would be sweeter were it not for those forgetful people screwing things

---

* Philippians 3:14: *I press toward the mark for the prize of the high calling of God in Christ Jesus.*

up for we who remembered. When Rush Limbaugh said "People forget," it was a way of flattering his audience. *You and me,* it said—as invisible hand bounces between puffed-out chests—*we know.* Those other people, they know *nothing.* And while all media outlets congratulate their audience on being part of a special club, something in this formulation sounded spittle-chinned to me and, though I dared not say it, unchristian. Listen to this style of rhetoric for too long and you lose the ability to affirm your beliefs (or yourself) in uncompetitive terms. As if wisdom grew more precious when contrasted to someone else's folly.

"You know I voted for McGovern," my father would say when it seemed that if we talked any longer we would alienate each other forever. He kept reaching out to me.

✦

When I traveled home and reported on my life, I showed off my new ability to flout the don't-arouse-envy rule.

I bumped into Ralph Lauren the other day, I said.

Wow, my mother would say.

"I mean I literally bumped into him," I'd clarify. "Almost knocked him over. It was a fashion week party in a tent and there was this carpet that hadn't been tacked down properly, I guess, and anyhow, my friend hadn't given me any notice—he just said be ready in a half hour and so there I was in skanky jeans and high-heeled boots and anyhow, wasn't watching where I was walking and tripped on loose carpet and oops—there he was. He's very tan, Ralph Lauren. Almost orange."

Or I'd say, "You know, four of my ex-boyfriends have gone on to date non–native English speakers. Maybe there's a lesson for me in there somewhere."

"Gosh, your life is so much more exciting than mine," she'd reply.

She says this as we sit at a cafeteria and cake shop in St. Paul.

Across the street was once Odegaard's Bookstore, where during furloughs we stocked up on English paperbacks, and that's why we liked lunch here, because it reminded us of a time when more outcomes seemed possible. Instead of replying I scrape wild rice off a chunk of chicken breast. If I denied that fashion week parties were more exciting than commuting to White Bear Lake, I'd insult her intelligence. She filled the silence herself.

"Dave bought a new house today."

"Oh yah?"

"Patricia was interested in downsizing, but now I guess they're not. They'll still have about thirty-five hundred square feet."

The cadences of her boss's spending habits are familiar: Dave now stored $3 million worth of golf memorabilia in the office. Once he stopped by a Jaguar dealership on the way home from work and wrote out a check right then and there for an XJ sedan. Her first order of business every morning was listening to the dictation tapes Dave left behind daily. *Karen, will you pull up Ferguson's file . . . Karen, I need to check the boat registration because Chad . . . Karen, there's this new kind of decaf . . . Karen, Chad was in another little fender bender, so . . .* My mother opened the Visa statements every month and made sure they were paid on time.

"Other than that, things are pretty boring. I live vicariously through you," she says.

I worry I've gone too far, so I mention that I still have the black wool gabardine suit she bought me my first year in New York. Funny, we agree, how Banana Republic had let quality considerations slide, because you used to be able to get good stuff there, durable stuff.

✦

We visited Marian in her assisted living apartment. She pretended it was possible I was still a virgin.

"I pray for you by name every day," she said, handkerchief squeezed in one hand, my hand squeezed in the other, eyes squeezed tight in concentration behind wire-rimmed glasses.

"Every day. I pray for you every day," she repeated. "And I just love you so much, and I want good things for you, and I want you to know the Lord and . . ." She let her sentence trail off. That I lived in New York City and had never been mugged, raped, or otherwise physically harmed she attributed to God's grace entirely, giving no credit to dropping crime rates or the policing strategies of former NYPD chief William J. Bratton. Those were details of marginal significance. Not the real story. She stomached my rebellion because they hoped the light would eventually come back on in me.

✦

Back in New York: Someone tells me how a friend of his, etc., etc., had overheard Richard Nixon comment on his admiration for Barbara Bush. *I like that woman; she really knows how to hate* was Nixon's remark, and I kept this one to myself because my mother would think I was relishing an insult leveled against Mrs. Bush when in fact I was only relieved to hear in it evidence that powerful people know things about other powerful people, and one way to get power was to amass enough data that you left the powerful with no choice but to welcome you into their ranks.

Know enough and the world would give you what you wanted, and no loyalty was uncomplicated. For a few mean seasons, this is the gospel I spread.

✦

Amy met Mark when he was the TA for an extension class she took on the early Christian Church. They were married in their living room. The officiant knew both bride and groom well. He spoke of how they debated until all hours and took coffee with startling quantities of half-and-half. I was asked to read a passage from Ruth, an unorthodox choice for a wedding because it concerned a widow's loyalty to her dead husband's mother: "Don't urge me to leave you or to turn back from you," Ruth says to her mother-in-law. "Where you go I will go, and where you stay I will stay. Your people will be my people and your God my God. Where you die I will die, and there I will be buried." Mark had grown up in a devout evangelical family who would only pay for Bible college and no other, and so when he tossed their fire and brimstoning aside, he never looked back except to spit.

Champagne popped. The dance party was relegated to the study but when the rain cleared, we took the celebration outside to get dripped on by wet leaves. Amy spun around in her short white dress and made fish lips at people snapping pictures, and the next day they'd be off to the Greek islands of Santorini and Patmos and somewhere in Turkey—they hadn't decided where. They had specified no gifts, just the presence of select loved ones.

Later visits to their ground-floor apartment in Cambridge centered on the kitchen table. Wine poured and scotch cracked ice cubes until three in the morning, when we'd retire and wake to more mugs of coffee with half-and-half and a hungover contented stroll down Mass Ave to the Harvard Book Store remainder tables. The first thing Amy had liked about Mark was his irreverence. Growing up with fundamentalists had turned him staunchly atheist. He held nothing sacred save Camel Lights and rhetoric and zooming around on a scooter in Greece. *You must leave Athens as soon as humanly possible*, he'd say, swallowing Jameson. *I mean it. Get out to the towns.* He could talk circles around anyone at any stage of intoxication while cleaning his glasses with his untucked shirt. We all talked late into the night and agreed that the Hustad missionary upbringing, pleasant tinges of exoticism aside, had generally speaking been bad for us, and further that Midwestern evangelical know-nothingness had deprived us of the launch in life we deserved. *You*—Mark jabbed a finger in my direction—*should have gone to Yale. And that they were too church-minded to see that is unconscionable.* I nodded, enjoying having someone be so angry on my behalf.

I noticed that Amy's hands shook sometimes, and that he spoke sharply to her.

One Thanksgiving they beckoned me to Cambridge for the long weekend. They'd also invited a visiting scholar at Princeton whom Mark had recently met at an academic conference. No pressure, Amy told me, but they thought this British fellow and I might hit if off.

Early that day, Mark left to pick Damon up at Logan Airport, encountered traffic snarls and parking lots filled to capacity, then realized he'd forgotten Damon's cell phone number on a Post-it on his desk at work and so couldn't call Damon to inform him that he would be late, let alone tell him where to stand for a curbside pickup. He called Amy instead. I leaned on the counter and watched as she stirred a pot of turnip leek soup, phone held under her chin, asking gentle questions as to how she might help, growing agitation taking over her face. It seemed he wanted her to fix traffic. The line went dead after Mark's distinct and audible "Fuck off."

Amy placed the receiver back down on the counter as if it were fragile. I asked her what possessed him to speak to her that way. She wondered if she had said the right thing, or perhaps blanked on an obvious solution that might have been more helpful to him. Amy refused to speak to me about it, him, or herself for weeks afterward. *Everything's great*, she'd say. They had spectacular fights it's true. But the fights always ended and ended well.

"Not cute enough" was my verdict on Damon, a gratuitously snotty dismissal that enraged Mark, I later found out.

✦

Mother's Day 2005 our father did something unusual. It was imperative, he said, that we visit Vivian. We hadn't seen her in years and who knew how long we had left. Amy and I booked connecting flights through Chicago so we could travel the last leg to Lincoln together.

I saw her standing a few gates down, arm clutched over her carry-on. She was already looking in my direction but didn't move toward me. She stood still. From one gate's length away I sensed that this standing still served to buy time. We hugged the one-armed hug of airport arrivals and her chin started wobbling. Hi. Hi. She suggested white wine. I looked at my watch. It was not yet noon. "Sure," I said. First sip down, she confessed that things with Mark were worse than she'd let on. Kicking and hair pulling. Her head through the window. Sometimes she slept wearing pants, her debit and credit cards and driver's license in her back pocket, because on nights he was excessively agitated she figured she might have to run, and there wouldn't be time to get dressed. The worst details she delivered in her most precise diction—clipped syllables as hedges against humiliation. To control shaking fingers she played with her wedding ring.

The flight to Lincoln was by all appearances uneventful. Beige tray tables, mild turbulence. She dropped her voice even further and talked until landing.

That afternoon she repeated every detail for our parents. The scenery now changed to a second-floor room at the Candlewood Suites, the hum of an old cooling unit in the background. We stood for the entire conversation because it is difficult to sit when someone speaks of their high tolerance for pain. We urged her not to return to Boston. She could come to New York with me, return to Minneapolis with them, she had options. No, she said, she'd be fine. She could handle this. *Like hell*, I said. *No really*, she said. *But Amy*, our parents said. She'd be fine, she said.

The set of her mouth told us the argument was over. That evening as she changed out of her shirt I glimpsed dark brown bruises along the length of her spine. *Oh my God*, I said. These she did not wish to discuss.

Her return to their apartment in Cambridge did not go as well as she'd hoped. Tuesday she called the police and Mark was taken into custody, and three days later he was arrested on the charges of assault and battery with a dangerous weapon, possession of a firearm without a Firearms Identification Card, and intimidation of a witness. Amy herself was the witness who had allegedly been intimidated. My parents flew in. I took the Acela. We talked about packing up her belongings, stood next to her in the courthouse hallway.

The charges were eventually dismissed without prejudice. Amy would not testify against Mark, and without her cooperation the district attorney had no case. Amy stood outside the hearing room and said that she fully realized that Mark needed help, but she did not think criminal prosecution or jail time would help him. They continued living together.

Over the next year, my parents received many angry phone calls. Amy was furious with us for having come to Cambridge that day on some pathetic hysterical misguided rescue mission. She yelled at them for not having supported her more as she started her career in Boston, for having let her attend that dumb Christian college, for never having liked Mark. She said she had wanted to stay in Holland for another year to qualify for Dutch citizenship and attend Leiden University, but they hadn't let her.

My parents had no memory of this.

Amy stopped visiting me in New York. This was not supposed to be the end of her story, and this I knew because we had written it together: affable husband with bad eyesight, a boy and a girl child, a leafy New England home, a tangle of rain boots in the mud room.

Family members assured me they were praying for Amy. One wrote a letter in longhand to Amy, five pages of thoughtfully articulated reasons for why Amy should leave Mark and at the bottom of the sixth an affirmation of grace. In grace, all things were possible.

I wondered if certain men have a knack for targeting women

who—let's say, despite throwing off all surface affiliation to Christianity—have a hard time saying *To hell with you*. Meanwhile people had so many suggestions. Had Amy read the books on domestic violence? Did she understand how high the recidivism rates were for men who refused treatment? Was she in possession of these facts? Had I shown her that *New York Times* article about that recent murder-suicide in midtown Manhattan? The assumption was that the right information delivered at the right time would set her free.

Via email Mark asked Amy's family for forgiveness. Could we forgive him for being such a wretched ass? We could, came back three responses. But that proved not to be the response Mark wanted, or so it seemed when those replies went unreplied to.

For months Amy's emails were pored over for signs she was preparing to leave.

Was this a case of excess forgiveness? I wondered. Was her problem that she forgave too much? Or that in their ongoing cycles of damage and reconciliation they missed the part of forgiveness where both the forgiver and the forgiven agree to put things behind them, to do better next time? But in their arguments Mark forever pulled the past forward—you did *this* six months ago, did *that* last year, years earlier, look at you, all this evidence of how disappointing you are, all the way back to being born a Hustad. Amy described the process in a rare phone call late one night: When he was really in a mood to mock, our father became "Stuttering Stan," and I: euphemisms that placed me on some tenuous spectrum between harridan and slut, and Karen—well, it was hard to condemn her, but the essential message was *You ought to be ashamed*.

In a box I find a letter that sixteen-year-old Amy wrote to Marian. She mentions a library book she'd checked out during one of our fundraising furloughs. She'd forgotten to return it and now she was back in Holland, Aunt Laura had received the overdue notice from the library, and for the life of her, Amy wrote, she couldn't remember where she'd left it. *Pygmalion*. That was the book.

Well, that's laying it on a bit thick, I thought. This was a ridiculous thing to think because it wasn't as if Amy's reading *Pygmalion* equated to her trying to make a point—about wanting to be some fair lady of a different class. Sometimes an overdue library book is just an overdue library book.

When we heard from Amy, which was every few months, we'd hear of ongoing fights. Mark's latest obsession was Campus Crusade for Christ, an evangelical organization focused on college students. Campus Crusade really pissed Mark off, and he wanted Amy to make it go away. That's an unreasonable request, we'd tell Amy—not really something that's within your power to change. *I know*, she said, and it's not like we were ever directly affiliated with Campus Crusade.

Another email gave me the sense that she was being prodded to continue identifying with other former MKs, many of whom Facebook informed us had become "part of the rightwing fringe that I abhor," she wrote. *Why explain that?* I wondered, as if I didn't share her politics, as if I didn't know that our father's rightward turns upset her. Absolutely everyone had become absolutely nutty, she continued. "It's honestly mindbending. I struggle to find a way to make sense of my beliefs and our past when everyone else that we grew up with has gone completely loony."

✦

I kept returning to Moberg's *Unto a Good Land* and particularly its passages on Scandinavian stoicism. The Swedes who migrated to Minnesota did not complain, no sir. Bread tasted better after you had carried a ninety-pound sack of flour for nine miles through virgin forest. To prevent the moral from being lost, Moberg has his Karl Oskar character explicitly declare his intention to refrain from speaking ill of circumstance in his first letter home to his parents. He instead writes:

Nothing happened on the journey and in August we arrived at our place of settling . . . Things go well for us and if health remains with us we shall surely improve our situation even though the country is unknown to us. I don't complain of anything, Kristina was a little sad in the beginning but she has now forgotten it.

Nonsense. Kristina lost two quarts of blood through her nose on the journey. The Americans they met suspected them of harboring cholera. One little girl in their party had died. Kristina was so homesick she was practically catatonic.

"You're pretty tough," Mark once remarked to Amy. So she told me during a rare week of contact. Funny, she thought— to be congratulated on what you will endure. The hour was late and her voice hoarse. *It is true, though*, she added. *I am pretty tough.* "Yes," I said. "Yes you are."

✦

Eventually Bonairian superstitions about surrounding a home with totems to ward off evil spirits began to sound smart to me. On one level, to think a goat skull would scare away an evil spirit was to assume evil spirits are easily spooked, which is comforting. On another level, there's so little effort involved, the means of securing your protection so flimsy, that surely no one really believed that it worked. The whole practice must have been a way to remind people of their powerlessness.

Or take the idea that you have to give the dead ample opportunity to leave your house. Throw doors and windows open and keep them open for seven days after a loved one dies, or the dead won't act dead, gray-haired Bonairians warned. So when Americans and city dwellers ask me how Amy wound up in the situation she's in, I shrug and say, "I don't know. Maybe she's haunted." Which elicits awkward silences, which is fine. When loneliness creeps in as the result of people's silence I indulge in thoughts like this: It's not that the unghosted aren't good people. I just don't know how to speak to them. It is simply that there are certain things that they do not understand and seem incapable of understanding.

✦

I'm in a hotel in the Recoleta area of Buenos Aires and the boyfriend's cell phone rings. We know it's early morning because sunlight is sneaking past the shades, but it's a pretty feeble attempt. Cue groans and fumbling, a trying to remember where he left the phone. His voice when he answers is all impatience. His assistant is on the line and wants him to know that she had received a call from his security company because the alarm in his apartment had been tripped. She was already dressed and on her way over and the police had been notified.

He looks over at me. Once this alarm went off when a stack of books fell over. Another time a mouse triggered the motion detector. Another time burglars tried drilling a hole in the door, but the apartment door, being owned by a paranoid man, was made of heavy metal. The wannabe burglars went away frustrated but left a reminder of their visit in the form of a fingertip-size dent.

The boyfriend hastens to put on a shirt. It's a jersey from an Eastern European soccer team, scratchy synthetic, all reds and blacks and eagle talons, so with his stubble and the gravel in his voice, he becomes hard to touch. I smile feebly. My great idea is this: I will help him feel okay about this possible burglary.

I try to signal empathy. I want to convey that I'm as worried as he is but this is difficult because I'm not. I know it took insurance appraisers with specialist skills a few days to add up all his art and prints and vases on old Provençal farmhouse tables. But I can't bring myself to speculate about what's happening to this stuff now, or much care. I check the corners of my eyes for sleep and try to concentrate on how much I like the gray in his stubble.

"Just things," I say. "They're just things."

In my mind I am making a helpful suggestion: at least nothing happened to a person he loved.

His gaze droops down to the carpet and I can tell he wishes sincerely I had never said this. In the corner of the room are three pairs of leather boots he has purchased for me, a jumble of beautiful boxes with coordinating tissue paper. Impractical kitten heel pumps in crocodile leather the color of dried blood. A new purse to wean me off the canvas totes that had become my default handbags after a couple of lean work years. I teared up upon receiving the first pair of boots—the shock of how easily money brought relief. The old boots they were to replace were so undesired that putting them on felt like failure that would unspool into failures, plural, possibly permanent.

Just things?

The boyfriend is too kind and tired to say what he's thinking, which is that I clearly hadn't thought this through. If I was going to start moralizing about how we shouldn't store up treasures here on earth . . . well, scratch that. What he was thinking was: *You are inconsistent, babe.*

But it was clearly one or the other in my view, the things we carry or people. That nothing be lost was not on the menu.

✦

I developed a theory: Amy's story was a consequence of mid-century American evangelicals' failure to anticipate that using mass media to spread the Gospel would make Christianity less popular, not more. They thought God would take their efforts and not only supplement but multiply them, as Jesus had done with the loaves and the fishes, and so after enough years of broadcast Christianity we'd be a fully Christian nation. But instead they aroused disgust, and Amy felt that disgust keenly.

I read *Left Behind*, a book I blamed more than most. *Here's the thing*, its holy-roller protagonists say. Here's the thing: Christians had been too polite. Too quiet. Now they were reconsidering that strategy. One character expresses his sense that he's gonna have to step up his hollering about Jesus, uncomfortable though that idea makes him. Another chimes in: "I went through a few days of that, worried what people would think of me, not wanting to turn anybody off."

Yeah. And later: "I'm going to start becoming obnoxious, I'm afraid."

Then our hero—Rayford Steele—says of his college-educated, New Yorky, fancy-pants daughter, whose soul he's really worried about:

"I'm going to force her to make a decision. She'll have to know exactly what she's doing. She'll have to face what we've found in the Bible and deal with it."

Because soon, Rayford knows, the elite, the well-educated, the ambitious, and the successful would eventually succumb to the truth. They could no longer "intellectually ignore" it.

Yeah, I think, *good luck with that*. When I brushed my teeth, I attacked them as if each tooth was coated in tar and spat out the toothpaste loud, catching my reflection in the bathroom mirror to see red in my eyes, looking down to watch blood swirled with spit and Colgate creep down the sides of the sink.

✦

I finally figured out why "You deserve it" bothered me. It had bothered me because it was itself a statement of faith. People said "You deserve it" to reassure themselves and one another that our efforts are rewarded. Seeing as I had recently gotten rid of one faith, I didn't appreciate being asked to embrace another.

NEW YORK II

Gradual reorientation toward our past looked like knee-jerk defensiveness at first. I sit in front of a computer monitor in an over-air-conditioned New York Public Library and execute a keyword search for "Bonaire." Up pops one listing: the collected letters of Marion West, a native New Yorker who lived on Bonaire in the early eighties at the behest of the U.S. Bahá'í National Center, as temporary replacement for the permanent "pioneer" they had stationed there. Her job was to form friendships and wait quietly for the opportunity to share the teachings of Bahá'u'lláh and his unifying world faith of which Judaism, Christianity, Buddhism, and Islam were but precursors.

Marion West's account of how she spends her days on Bonaire is reassuringly familiar. She swims, stares at sunsets, writes long letters, is preoccupied with insects and spiders. TWR, however, she cannot stomach. "Trans World Radio—a radio church of the air—has one of its largest transmitters on Bonaire. They have a large staff, mostly Americans . . . They don't really do much proselytizing of the native people. They are rather clannish and make no effort to learn the local language. They are, indeed, rather negative about it—'Let them speak Spanish.'"

That Marie Antoinettish "Let them" did not sound quite

right to me, and neither did "Spanish," not least because a Spanish-speaking local wouldn't make a monolingual English-speaking American missionary's job any easier than Dutch or Papiamento did. In a later letter West tells her husband that Bonaire locals lost their usual genial demeanor when contemplating both missionaries and boorish capitalists.

"While they are the nicest, most gentle of people (in Bonaire, at least) they have very harsh things to say about the Trans World Radio people and the Dutch who come here to work in the oil industry and who, even after twenty years on the island, don't try to speak Papiamento. I think that my blundering but sincere efforts to learn has done much to endear me, and the Faith, to the Bonairians."

Explicit proselytizing is not the Bahá'í pioneer's usual MO. Still, after a few months of Bonaire living, West decides she could be doing more in the way of outreach and she places an ad in *Amigoe*, a Curaçao newspaper:

ONE WORLD
ONE RELIGION
ONE MANKIND
Are you interested?
For information write:
BAHA'I INFORMATION CENTER
Box 33 – Bonaire

It runs daily for a week. She ran the ad in English, she explained to people back home, so she'd be able to handle the responses. Ha, dumb reflexes snap. Gotcha.

✦

Some days a devout atheist leaned in to tell me that the eradication of religious sentiment would mark a huge advance for mankind. We were collections of atoms and had consciousness, but that was it. *Religion and bigotry are two sides of the same coin*, he'll say. *Only those suffering from arrested development believe in God.*

One conversation about how eradicating religion would improve the world took place at a German-style beer garden on Avenue C in the East Village. My upstairs neighbor published a quarterly arts magazine that billed itself as GLOBAL. CREATIVE. PROGRESSIVE and he quickly took our conversation into *If there is an Auschwitz, then there cannot be a God* territory. Dylan did not know many religious people personally but had heard their campaign speeches. Large-scale human suffering meant God cannot possibly be all-powerful and loving, because if he were, innocents would not be mowed down with quite the frequency that they were. From there it was only sentences before he was remarking upon all the lives lost in religion's name. *9/11. The religious wars.* He hadn't known many Christians but had seen the ones on TV, the ones who spoke of God as a great big castrator in the sky, the enemy of all pleasure and independent thinking.

He was handsome and wearing an off-white linen shirt. I didn't want to argue so said, "You know, I really shouldn't order white wine at a beer garden" and stared over his shoulder at the housing projects across Avenue C and remembered that conversation with my father about how warehousing people of the same socioeconomic class together was a bad idea.

Dylan believed that we, meaning humans, were improving and would only continue to make better choices if not for religious superstitions. But I didn't appreciate how little I agreed until he asked if what had happened to my sister—and the fact that I hadn't seen her in three years and counting—had changed my perception of God. "No," I heard myself say. "It changed my perception of people."

He brushed brown bangs from his eyes. More loudly I added that my appetite for destruction reared its head every forty-eight hours, took a great mental struggle to subdue, and that if more people made life choices like mine we'd all starve.

Unlike my grandfather Orville I do not raise muskmelon from seed and do not know how.

"It's true, though," I say. "My parents' generation—at least early on—were always saying *Praise the Lord!* And it had a tone of exclamation points, happy, hands in the air, all that. And now we have *What Would Jesus Do?*, which seems to presume, uh, that the person asking is *capable* of doing what Jesus would do, which, I don't know, seems presumptuous."

Within a month the upstairs neighbor left for a vacation in Costa Rica and Nicaragua and decided to stay there. Airbnb allows him to sublet his apartment to tourists, so being tired of New York nets him $1,000 a month. For weeks afterward I thought of how I'd respond to his religion-ruins-everything comment: *Yes, and let's get rid of this whole "money" thing, too, because money seems to up the body count also.* Or: *What about car insurance? Why not not believe because car insurance exists? Toddler beauty pageants?* I listened to an audience member at a book reading propose to the author—whose book was about some evangelicals' belief that God spoke to them—that believing in God was like having an imaginary friend, or schizophrenia. *As if social media company stock valuations didn't rest on our appetite for imaginary friends,* I protest mutely. "Interesting idea" is the author's reply to the schizophrenia assertion.

✦

My father has lost interest in defending religious conviction. He lifts his hands in the manner of a man surrendering to the cops. His voice is tinged with exasperation.

"I don't try to defend the faith anymore," he says. "I just don't."

"Why?" I ask. "Why not?"

"Well, I came to the conviction some years ago that apologetics was a worthless exercise," he said. "You know? So what, who gives a crap? The fact that I could put up a great, great, wonderful defense . . . What good does it do?"

His nose has gotten longer, his posture more hesitant. We argue the day after Election Day 2008.

"Obviously I'm disappointed in the results," he said over the phone. He said Obama was just another Chicago thug. I replied that the McCain campaign had hardly clothed itself in honor. Conversation devolved from there. A few days later, my mother called me to say that she was sorry for not calling me on election night, when so many New Yorkers streamed into the streets to celebrate. They had lived through so many election nights that this one didn't strike them as anything special. She hadn't realized how exciting the outcome would be for some people, she said.

"Just another Chicago thug" was not something an earlier Stan Hustad would have said. Perhaps Limbaugh was his punk rock, the latest manifestation of his desire to unsettle.

We didn't speak for a while, then months later there's another phone call and we're discussing the 2009 economic stimulus package. My father was not impressed with what he perceived as Democratic boasting about having saved jobs.

"When people give me this crap about how we saved all the cops and teachers, you know . . . bullshit."

"Huh?"

"They say we saved all these jobs."

"Who said what," I pressed.

"Well," he said, "whether it's a political leader, whether it's a senator, or Valerie Jarrett, or anyone talking about the stimulus package, they say 'We saved all these jobs' . . . And that term 'saved' is obviously strange but . . . well, you know, a lot of teachers' jobs shouldn't be saved."

He could remember dozens of ineffectual teachers. Bad teachers losing their jobs would be a good thing, he said.

We moved on to New York City's "rubber room," a system in which teachers removed from their classrooms for alleged misconduct continue to report to work at a central holding tank / naughty corner as they wait for their appeal to be heard. They work on crossword puzzles or screenplays while drawing a full teaching salary. Some stay in the rubber room for years. As my father and I talked I found myself defending the rubber room, which surprised me. It's one of those situations where administrators just opted for the least worst option, I said. These teachers couldn't be in the classroom but couldn't be fired in violation of their employment contract, so the rubber room it was until contracts could be renegotiated and—

"Assholedom persists, then," my father concluded.

"Yes," I say.

He has come to believe that corruption and mediocrity are as human as cooing at babies, but that some people at some point chose to stop being mediocre. Others wanted to remain mediocre, and that was their business. It only became a problem when well-meaning but misguided softies—liberals—conspired to support them in their mediocrity, but at a remove, via the instrument of government.

He believed it was not the government's job to distribute food to the hungry, because when bureaucrats fed the hungry the act was sapped of its nurturing power. It became a *Here's your check, here are your papers, see you in a month* type of thing. There was no rebirth, just endless repetition.

He believed secular liberal arguments ignore the truth that all difficulties had a spiritual element. He believed nothing could be fixed through policies and systems, and certainly not through institutions. Intellectuals regarded evil as some kind of error. Gather more info and you won't commit the error. He couldn't believe that.

He believed the comfortably secular upper middle class had a habit of publicly endorsing lifestyles that worked fine for people with money, but rarely for people with little. The permissiveness possible in their lives was not such a good idea for people more precariously situated. Take their position on single parenthood, for instance. Liberals also placed too much emphasis on *freedom from*. They were stuck on the delights of doing things previously forbidden and never considered that any radical loosening of restrictions gave rise to equal and opposite obligations. One day you're allowed to have sex outside of marriage, the next day you're expected to. One day porn is fine, the next day you're a prude for objecting to it.

But abortion, his imagined opposition would say. *Yes*, he would reply, it's true I don't want teenagers pregnant and I don't want them having abortions, either. Here's why: Every human wants to come into being. Every thing, in fact, wanted to persist in being. Bugs, ants, mice, rats, all indifferent to the hostile forces surrounding them that want them extinguished. Life would insist on living.

Plastic bags, too. Once a thing is made, it's a lot of work to get rid of it. No one could deny that. Very little in creation slunk conveniently away once it wasn't wanted. Even art insisted on coming into being, he said.

I hesitated to say otherwise. I didn't know what he meant.

So we say Jesus was God's son, he said, but we're also saying that Jesus represents a fundamental truth of a universe that privileges incarnation. Ask a creative person and they will sometimes tell you: those paintings needed to be made. They all but demanded, *Make me*. So . . . for any person to argue that we did not choose to be born was assuming facts not in evidence.*

---

*His thoughts on the subject were inspired by Dorothy L. Sayers's *The Mind of the Maker*:

> The resistance to creation which the writer encounters in his creature is sufficiently evident, both to himself and to others—particularly to those others who have the misfortune to live with him during the period when his Energy is engaged on a job of work . . . Almost equally evident, however, though perhaps less readily explained or described, is the creature's violent urge to be created . . . That a work of creation struggles and insistently demands to be brought into being is a fact that no genuine artist would think of denying. Often, the demand may impose itself in defiance of the author's considered interests and at the most inconvenient moments. Publisher, bank-balance, and even the conscious intellect may argue that the writer should pursue some fruitful and established undertaking; but they will argue in vain against the passionate vitality of a work that insists on manifestation . . . Because of this,

Besides, "pro-choice" seemed to him prissy, as if a life free of life-altering mishap, a life in which your march toward American Express platinum cards was unimpeded, no untidy gaps on your CV, was achievable. Or even desirable.

Still, he was often surprised how eagerly people misread scripture. The Bible says *The sins of the fathers are visited on the sons to the third and fourth generation.* How could God dictate that? So mean! Punishing people for what their parents did? Well, no. *The sins of the fathers*—that was simply a description of animal life. That was how the world worked.

✦

My father tells his clients they will have to make their own way. Those jobs are never coming back, and any sense of security you clung to in the past has been revealed for what it was all along—an illusion. The clients he's best at attracting are intrigued by his missionary past. He says that he tries to "be present" to his clients, by which he means he provides sustained eye contact and leans in. He lets them finish their sentences when they struggle to do so.

Wasn't it strange, he continues, that the words "problem" and "solution" aren't to be found in the Bible? Neither is the word "happiness." These were not terms a Christian should really be thinking in, and that they were so dominant in our cultural conversation was further proof that mainstream American culture was thoroughly secularized. So secularized that even Christians talked as if all problems had solutions and all solutions addressed real problems.

He was still bothered by the fact that a person could make more money lighting pornographic films than she could growing corn, but if moral reprobates used their freedom to wreak

---

the artist ought, above all men, to be chary of basing his philosophy of life on the assumption that "we are brought into this world by no choice of our own." That may be so, but he has no means of proving it, and the analogy of his own creative experience offers evidence to the contrary.

spiritual havoc, so be it. The same freedom that allowed us to do good work allowed us to behave terribly.

For a while he thought about a book on performance coaching that would teach prospective coaches how to arrive at a "deep aliveness" that helped them attract influential clients, a book that would be supplemented by an online coaching service linked with passwords from the book—similar to what Marcus Buckingham did in *Discover Your Strengths*. One day he met a gentleman who persuaded him to fly to São Paolo to speak at a conference. All my father had to do was secure a visa for Brazil, pack a sports coat, and come prepared to talk. The Brazilian would take care of the airfare.

Travel arrangements weren't completed until the week before the conference, and this delay forced bad connections. He would fly to Newark, land at 11:00 p.m., and depart from JFK at 7:45 the following morning. He didn't want to spend too much on a hotel for those few hours. Maybe he'd sleep in the airport, he said—he'd done it before.

I did not see him on his short sweep through town but I received an email from him the night he landed in São Paolo. He reported that he had been put up in a very modest little hotel north of the city. By "very modest" I took him to mean spartan, not too many bugs. He had not received an agenda yet but the man who had organized the convention was a dynamo. *It was a real adventure*, he wrote.

✦

These days my parents touch each other more than at previous points in their marriage. They give reassuring pats. They hug like survivors stepping off a lifeboat. In sunset tones on the patio swing, in the hour before my mother starts dinner, they discuss how to think about what happened to us.

My father decided to write Amy letters that confessed to some failings. He had been too distracted in Holland and often since, he said. He wrote them by hand in his long, swooping cursive and walked them out to the mailbox, raised the flag, and waited.

They did not have the effect he was hoping for. He cried but decided to keep going. One day he calls and his voice breaks. "I loved you," he said. "But I didn't fight for you. Maybe I grew up in a culture that was too pacifistic, too feminine, too pastoral, or therapeutic, but I didn't fight for you. And I'm very sorry for that. I'm very sorry."

My mother can't make up her mind whether it was okay to feel angry about Amy's situation. She thinks of verses in Proverbs like *Don't let the sun go down on your anger.* At a deeper level, she also thinks that forgoing anger was something God generally preferred we do. Forgive and ask for forgiveness, etc.

My father suggests that Jesus himself got upset about the moneychangers in the temple kicking over tables and sending trinkets scattering to the floor. Some anger was perfectly fine, my father proposed. More than justified.

But my mother was trying to talk herself out of this anger with the help of a women's Bible study group that met every Monday. They'd been talking about unanswered prayer. *What did the speaker have to say about that?* I asked.

Sometimes prayer goes unanswered because we're praying for the wrong things, my mother said. *Sometimes there is some sin in our lives that we haven't dealt with.* In all there were five things that blocked answers to prayer. I suggested we make it simpler and say that sometimes we got what we wanted, sometimes not, and either way it's beyond our control. Couldn't a person imagine that when Jesus said "Thy will be done" he meant it more as a general acknowledgment of submission to greater powers, as a *Masterpiece Theatre* butler might say "As you wish!" And perhaps that implied Christians shouldn't be so obsessed with God's will, but adopt a more Zen approach, instead of this odd fixation on What God Wants for Me. Maybe the point of prayer was to change the person who prays.

We move on. She says people have different interpretations.

Her friend Kathy's mother, for instance, wasn't a Christian and is now dead but Kathy still believes she will see her mother in heaven.

"Huh," I say. "What do you think?"

Silence. A staring into the wineglass.

"What do you think?" I ask again. "Do you think I'm going to hell?"

She nods ever so slightly. Silence. Both of us staring into wineglasses. Then— She doesn't— She doesn't think, oh—

"Just what I was raised to believe," she says. She continues: She didn't know. She hadn't really thought about these things too much. Then the conversation ends because she has to go.

A week later she calls to tell me she'd thought about it some more. What she guessed she actually believed, she said, is that once saved, always saved. She was also trying to stockpile less food, she said, just as I'd suggested, and Amy, too. She knew she kept too much food in the house, and she was really trying to be better about that. *I'm trying*, she said. *I'm really trying to be better.*

✦

Many months passed after Marian died before I admitted her prayers had buoyed me. Before I glibly joked—yes, sure, couldn't hurt in a New Agey sending-good-vibes sense. I didn't believe hopes spoken eyes-shut by a woman resident of a Minnesota nursing home affected my daily experience in New York.

Once she was gone, however, I missed knowing that she was daily pleading my case. She wouldn't have felt the need to do that, you see, if evidence of God's love were so easily grasped. If God could be counted on to remember her granddaughters and value their safety, she'd need only ask God once. Instead she prayed every day, each of us by name.

So daily prayer was acknowledgment that her God's attitude toward his creations was like any artist's. Some days he swelled with disgust at how clumsy and fat-fingered it all was. Her God was a poet tempted to throw his manuscript pages into the fire. A painter who paints over his old paintings.

In the story of Job, Job is a good man who suffers setback after setback, humiliation upon horrible tragedy, and he appeals to God: *Why is this happening to me?* God's response is devastating: "Where were you when I laid the foundations of the earth?"

Then in the Gospels, we're told Jesus had been on the cross for nine hours when he cried out. Psalm 22: *My God, my God, why have you forsaken me?* Silence. There's no answer.

So there was Marian saying: Look here. Pay attention. Look how wonderful your creation is. I don't need an answer but please don't you dare lose sight of these girls.

✦

I asked my mother, my father, Amy: Do any of you remember how the kids at school—Bonaire, I mean—thought that the white splotch on dad's forearm meant he had tangled with some bad juju? (Stan's left forearm had a large spot of unpigmented skin, unnoticeable after a Minnesota winter but very evident after a few days of Caribbean sun.) The spot looked like a splash of hydrogen peroxide. Or else, and more likely, these kids thought, he'd been grabbed by the arm and pulled into a corner by an evil spirit. Why would the spirits want to mess with him? Maybe he messed with *them*, and this scar was his trophy. *Or* he was zapped while just minding his own business.

No one else remembered this.

✦

I asked my mother about the JCPenney job she gave up to become a missionary. Did she like it? *Sure*, she said. Every day brought a caller who'd found a new reason to be upset. She was good at it, she said. Being a friendly voice of reason on the other end of the telephone line.

MORE THAN CONQUERORS

"And I only dealt with people who were having trouble with their bills."

"Any memorably belligerent callers?"

"Well, the most difficult people to deal with were ministers and lawyers."

"Really?"

"Well, you know, when I was growing up, ministers got a ten percent discount. We always went to JCPenney for Easter shoes because we got a discount there. I don't know when that was discontinued, maybe sometime in the sixties, but anyway, it was hard for them to adjust, I think. Pastors were used to being treated differently."

Then she had to hang up because she was running late for work. Before goodbye she added this: (1) the first computer she worked with filled an entire room, and (2) she once appeared in the JCPenney employee magazine. She'd kept it. She would mail it to me.

"We make a real effort to answer a customer's inquiry as quickly as possible or to let her know within forty-eight hours of our progress," she was quoted in an article on their credit program's billing inquiry rapid response times. "Each of us is held personally responsible for any late replies."

The accompanying black-and-white photograph depicts her indicating a line of text on a computer screen with a pencil. The article further boasted that JCPenney did not profit from credit card service charges and actually lost money on the program. Other pages of *Penney News* announce the pastels for spring 1973: cool blue, frosty pink, creamy yellow, mint julep, icy beige. Swimsuits would be skimpy but caftans were "in." Also, customers needed to be educated about new federal standards for flame-retardant children's sleepwear. On the last page the winners of their sixth annual awards for writers in the women's interest field of journalism are announced. That year's $1,000 top honor went to Ralph Nader for work published in the *Ladies' Home Journal*, and Nader received his reward at a lunch reception held at New York's Regency Hotel. For the next several months I entertain the dream that Amy would have been better off in a country where Ralph Nader, JCPenney, the Regency Hotel, and my mom were on the same team.

✦

Former missionaries I tracked down had motivations similar to my parents'—to be unusual, to have fewer regrets over things undone. One couple we knew in Holland mentioned how their daughter, fourteen at the time, had been molested by one of the Intracare students, and underwent years of counseling when they returned to the States. As the wife told me this, she kept saying "The gentleman who caused this to happen"—never using the phrase "child molester." She was either extremely polite or using stilted grammar to reinforce the space between a man and his sins. (Perhaps it was her approximation of grace. A photocopy of a photocopy of a photocopy. *The gentleman who caused this to happen.* Someday we would experience God's grace in full, but in the meantime, she was to extend it herself in dribs and drabs and in shying away from labels, from placing a period at the end of anyone's story.)

I looked up John Till, whom we'd known on Bonaire. He tells me that in his family, missionary was a career choice like any other. For a while he worked as a youth minister at an English-speaking Baptist church in a suburb of The Hague. He returned to the States and wanted to stay in radio, "but don't let it be a country station," he pleaded to God.

Ten years later he lost his job as the straight man on a country station morning drive-time show. Now he teaches ninth and tenth graders categorized as behavior problems at a North Carolina high school. He likes talking to his students about disillusionment, he says. "It hurts, I tell them." But it was good to have lost illusions, he says. A few years ago he came across the concept of "third-culture kids," formulated by 1960s psychologists seeking to capture the peculiar sensibilities of children who had spent years in foreign countries, mixing elements of their birth culture with thought habits of the culture they had been plunked down into. MKs and military brats, mainly. Ask them "Where are you from?" and they couldn't give the expected one-noun answers. They were perpetually one beat off. "One of the interesting things about the concept," he says, "is that in order to be a third-culture kid, you have to be with your parents. Spending time abroad on your own, like on a foreign exchange program or at boarding school, won't do it." Studies show that members of third-culture families spend more time staring at one another than is typical in families that stay put, if only because one another's faces are the only constant as they swap scenery every few years.

Joan and Skip Britton, retired missionaries, had met in Monte Carlo, moved to Bonaire, back to Monte Carlo, and spent their last missionary years in Bratislava. They now lived in a small three-bedroom rambler ten minutes off I-10 in central Tennessee. Over coffee cake I asked about their time in Bratislava. *Cheap opera tickets*, Joan replied. *So much cheaper than Vienna. Great grocery shopping at Carrefour.* The ledge inside their front picture window held twelve pots of African violets. *Skip's handiwork*, Joan says. She talked me through the contents of her dining room curio cabinet: dishware from Italy, Russian dolls, seashells, a Japanese tea set given to her mother by a Norwegian soldier after World War II. Skip kept in shape by swimming laps at the community pool and by playing the occasional tennis game. She kept busy in a book club and a writing group.

She escorted me down the narrow hall to a tiny guest room with a double bed, nightstand, desk and desk chair, two lamps, a magazine rack filled with thumbed-through copies of *Reader's Digest*. "Everything in this house was either a gift or bought for a dollar," she said. The next morning Skip channel-surfed between Fox News and a Serena Williams match, the TV on mute and a leather-bound Bible open on his lap. I asked him what he was reading. "The first chapter of Ecclesiastes," he said.

Joan's favorite Bible verse (I asked) was Psalms 16:11: *You will make known to me the path of life, you will fill me with joy in your presence, with eternal pleasures at your right hand.* She felt this required explanation. She had grown up Christian, she said. First in Bay Ridge, Brooklyn, then northern New Jersey. Whenever her family ventured into Manhattan she felt humbled by grittiness. Her fifteen-year-old self decided that her Christian testimony would be more meaningful if she had a rough-and-tumble story like that told in *The Cross and the Switchblade*, in which a juvenile delinquent gang member turns to Jesus and goes on to minister to other alienated youth. She thought her testimony about the saving grace of God would be more credible if she could similarly speak to having been spared some dingy fate. The discovery of Psalms 16:11 was encouraging because to her it said there was drama aplenty in being good. If she craved excitement, she would find it in fellowship with God.

✦

It's a very American idea, to think that parents are supposed to become less human for their children's sake. So I stumble upon a trick for helping me feel for my father whenever I pass through their TV room and Sean Hannity is on. I picture my father in that window of time soon after he grew a beard and voted for McGovern, not long after the summer of 1973, when he and my mother visited Europe's museums for the first time, when he decided that the kids of Rosemount High School needed to know a little art history. When he had first been handed the ninth grade civics class, the state-mandated curriculum was divided into three areas of concentration: American government, careers, and drivers ed. Because what did kids in semirural middle America need to know? How to drive, because they had no other way out of town unless they hitchhiked. How and when to vote. And once what remained of their parents' fields was paved over, assuming they didn't get themselves killed in Vietnam or driving down train tracks first, they would need to earn money. But this wasn't good enough for them. He knew that. Should these kids ever get out of town, they might hear certain names dropped. If they stood there blinking, mute, people would suspect no one had bothered to educate them properly. And there were simply things a person should know.

He mentions this on a visit to New York and the Metropolitan Museum of Art, early on a Saturday morning. We gravitated toward seventeenth-century paintings and the Rembrandts and Vermeers because we knew these paintings and the galleries were not so crowded. Georges de La Tour's *The Penitent Magdalen* is the painting that dislodged this recollection of his younger self. The list of paintings he gave his students was limited by the slides he could get his hands on. Most came from the Met. At quiz time he asked his students to identify the painter, the title of the painting, and the reasons why this painting was important. *This painting is not a foreign object*, he wanted his students to understand. *You are in this painting*.

I asked him where he found the slides.

"It's hard to remember how you looked for things before the Internet," he says. Then: the school basement.

So I picture my father schlepping to the basement, trolling the aisles of the AV storage room, and switching on a Kodak Carousel and aiming its beam at a wall uncluttered by storage shelves. The carousels came equipped with an internal fan that kept them from overheating. Maybe the fan muffled the strains of band practice seeping in through the duct vents. His steps echo hollow as he strides over to hit the switch plate and kill the overhead light. I imagine him feeling alone, in the way of a boy worried he'll be interrupted only to be scolded for wasting his time.

Among the slides he chose for the quiz: a Rembrandt self-portrait; El Greco's *View of Toledo*; Georges de La Tour's *Saint Joseph the Carpenter*. (The Saint Joseph of the title—Jesus's earthly father—is aging and gray-bearded, bent over his carpentry, sweat pooling under his eyes.)

I picture him rattling the slide tray because stuck trays resulted in melted slides. When rattling the tray doesn't help, he switches the carousel off and the room is tossed back into darkness and quiet.

Yank out the tray. Count to ten. Set it back in place.

"I found there was a deep ordinariness to life," he tells me years later. "Even though I'd been a good teacher, there was no way I could see myself saying, *Let's do this for twenty more years.*"

✦

Another gift is remembering Snap, Crackle, Pop, and finding this passage underlined in one of the dusty used books he buys online and reads over black coffee at 5:30 a.m., the hour before cable news is switched on and while untainted love still seems feasible: *Do not pray to bring things to pass; pray to see things that already are.*

Passages underlined in books. A universal reading list is all he really wants. If only, my father dreams, if only we all agreed on a reading list.

✦

For my mother I remember something about our past—something I remember snips of, mainly the visuals or the smells. The rest I fabricate and attach words to and see her young, younger than I am now.

Say furlough is over, and we're back on Bonaire, it's 1981, and she's down at the fruit boat. She never liked the fruit boat but liked it still less when memories of bright supermarket produce sections were fresh.

The fruit boat was a dinghy manned by two men who arrived from Venezuela on Mondays, tied themselves to the Kralendijk pier with a rope thick with tar residue and salt, and stayed until Friday, or until their dinged-up wooden crates were empty. They did not need to woo customers because they were the only fruit sellers in town. If you wanted bananas or oranges or *sorsaka*, you visited these skinny men with heavy eyelids. They closed up shop at sunset by throwing a tarp over the crates and refusing to hear your entreaties. The next morning, plantains were always browner and black flies more insistent. By Friday the smell of fruit pulp fermenting into alcohol, the smells of sweat, salt, urine, and men who slept in their clothes, swirled up and out onto the pier.

My mother hid her gag reflex well. She could tell they didn't like her. Occasionally she let the pushier of the two nudge her into buying more bananas than she wanted. Weekly she resolved to be friendlier. Part of the problem, she knew, was the rumors that TWR was somehow linked to the CIA. Part of the problem was that she was thought rich.

Being considered rich—what a strange feeling. A few weeks before one Bonaire Christmas she stopped by the airport customs office to collect a package from the States. The small square box contained a shiny ball of handblown beige glass wrapped in matching beige tissue paper. A Christmas tree ornament with a declared value of $75. Her cheeks flushed hot pink with irritation. First there was the duty she'd have to pay on $75. Then the raised eyebrows of the customs officials, the glint of disapproval that said *Look at this spoiled woman with this shiny bauble good for nothing.*

But how to explain to family and supporters both that $75 ornaments complicated all of life, even the purchase of overripe bananas on different days, she had no idea. Even to know which was worse—poverty itself or the tendency of people to misunderstand what you really need. She would pray for more eloquence.

✦

Amy, by the way, was student body president at her high school in Holland. I feel compelled to add this far, far too often. For graduation she wore a knee-length navy knit jersey dress that, like most eighties fashions, was slinky but not especially revealing. In addition to long sleeves, sewn into the tapered side seams at her ribs were two additional sleevelike extensions that wrapped around in front to belt the waist. She was, this dress announced, so cool.

No caps and gowns in Holland, she clarified as I watched her prepare for the party. "They don't do that here." No, I nodded, of course not. Why should they? Your own clothes are better.

The graduation ceremony took place in the evening, lit by candles. Amy's earrings dangled below her dirty-blond curls, grazed her shoulders, and caught the attention that ricocheted off the auditorium's walls and fell on her. She sat in front, punctuating her laughter with claps that did not seem Anne of Green Gablesish when she did it, but sophisticated. On her nightstand, those Simone de Beauvoir paperbacks. And I mention these things to good people when for a second they lose themselves and let it slip that they think, *Oh, that only happens to women who haven't been introduced to certain ideas, certain books, only happens to women with questionable taste.*

✦

One occasion Amy wants to remember: the Foreign Missions Club in London. So cheap that we got a room separate from our parents'. The Laura Ashley dresses, the night we stayed in while Mom and Dad went to the theater. We know now what we didn't know then. These extravagances were made possible by our parents' dipping into their $25,000 in savings from selling the house. So that just once we could feel the exhilaration of wanting and receiving the same day.

This, too: how she enjoyed having knowledge visitors did not. You could tell these visiting American adults that a person must close gates or the goats ate all the hibiscus flowers—anything red, really. They'd get a look that said, *Can't something be done?* and you'd know, no, goats have no regard for beauty, or maybe they did, so much so that they wanted to ingest it, but either way, don't worry, just close the gate and go swimming.

ELLUL Ellul did not grow up in a religious household, and while his mother dabbled in it, his father merely tolerated her feelings on the subject. As a teenager, Ellul preferred Marx because Marx's characterization of what ailed our society seemed uncomfortably accurate in the way only true things do. His delight in finding that somebody had anticipated all of his own thoughts regarding power, inequity, and work quickly wore off. Marx didn't seem to have much to say about the human heart. Ellul was beginning to think this was indicative of a deeper failing.

Preparation for school exams led him to Goethe's *Faust*. *Faust* led him to the New Testament and sentences like this from the book of John: *In him was life; and the life was the light of men. And the light shineth in darkness; and the darkness comprehended it not.*

Then God . . . did something. Ellul kept mum on details. He later revealed that he was twenty, and the experience was violent. "As violent as the most violent conversion you have ever heard of," he told an interviewer. Elsewhere he described it this way: Christ "imposed himself upon me." Once he intimated that his conversion bore strong similarities to the conversion of Saint Paul in the book of Acts—a God-despising man is knocked off his horse as a sudden strong light floods his retinas. He is temporarily blinded because God wanted his attention.

"I realized that God had spoken, but I didn't want him to have me," Ellul wrote. "I fled. This struggle lasted for ten years."

The belief that God was real was one thing. The belief that God's existence carried any personal implications came ten years later.

Once an interviewer asked Ellul if he saw any point to evangelism and missionary work, or conversion more generally, given that, as Ellul decided later in his career, everyone was saved. Did it make sense to venture out into the world to speak of Jesus Christ if no soul was condemned to hell? If peace awaited everyone, including the Buddhist, the Muslim, the atheist, why plug Christianity to the unconvinced? Take away the ultimate justification for evangelism—rescuing people from eternal torment—and you were left with little.

Ellul mulled this over for a moment. When he finally spoke, he admitted that he did continue to speak to people of Christ. He said such conversations were typically prompted by someone's confessing that he or she was in despair and did not see a way forward. Then he would speak of the source of his solace. This was rather different from the Spanish Inquisition, he said. Their MO had been "Be converted or I'll kill you." His own was more like, "It seems you want to kill yourself, so here's an idea that can help you escape the desire to kill yourself."

And that was the whole point of the Ten Commandments, he continued. They were not orders but a terse summary of the human condition. They began by acknowledging that everyone worshipped something but that people were inclined to worship stupid things. We were forever chasing things and people that did not belong to us. We were ungrateful. Give us something and we want more of it. Give us something else, and we glance over at what our neighbor was handed, and say, *Oooh, I need that, too*. We draw caricatures of other people in our heads, then pay more attention to those caricatures than to the individuals themselves.

So you have to see the Ten Commandments as promises, Ellul concluded, not as imperatives. They prod us to imagine the possibility of freedom from petty, stingy, sloppy, and narcissistic impulses. They prod us to believe it is possible to live more elegantly.

It was strange what had happened to the church, he added. (He was talking about the Reformed Church of France in the fifties, and how it withered.) Given that Christianity stressed the primacy of inner peace, as opposed to, say, institutional or structural solutions to the world's problems, Christians really ought to be the least ideological people. Because for them, everything except history was done. Second, Ellul continued, no political or social ideology could be gleaned from the Bible that was truer than other doctrines. That wasn't what the Bible was *for*. He believed the true consequences of Christian faith were courage, inventiveness, a radical ability to distance oneself from everyday objects and everyday opinions—everything, in short, that the powers of this world clung to white-knuckled.

But most Christians were *not* less ideologically encumbered than other people, not at all, and no one thought of Christians that way, and for good reason, he told his interviewer: most Christians failed at being Christians. In fact, every time he met with his friend Bernard Charbonneau, who was an atheist, he first had to listen to a torrential monologue of indictments against Christians, hear how intolerable Christians were, and how they betrayed everything Jesus stood for. This ranting out of the way, Ellul said, they could sit down to dinner.

✦

"Heaven and hell," my father writes in an email. "I am not sure they are places but positions and relationships."

POSTLUDE: HOME

And it's so forehead-smacking obvious now, but I couldn't see a thing when it happened.

I was at my cubicle desk, twenty-six years old, convinced the department bosses thought I was not smart enough for the job, and possibly insufficiently dedicated. I called home on my lunch hour and my father answered. I told him I was unhappy as well as increasingly convinced my boss was right and I was not cut out for this work.

"I really just want to quit," I said.

"Then you should quit," my father said.

"But I don't have anything else lined up," I said.

Even over the phone I could sense his shrug.

"Of course," he continued. "People say you should never quit a job unless you have another one lined up. But people say all kinds of things. If you've reached a point where you are doubting your own abilities, just quit."

"But—"

"We won't let you starve," he said.

He had never scored high in the risk aversion department, he continued. He suspected I was the same.

So I gave notice. That same week, my boyfriend broke up with me and my landlady told me that she needed my apartment for her brother who was getting out of some kind of situation in

Puerto Rico and could I please be out by the end of the month. It's really perfect, I told concerned coworkers. It's perfect because three problems at once saves you from worrying excessively about any one. I took private solace in being so—uniquely, I fantasized—my own person.

When in reality, unrecognized by me at the time, I was no more and no less than a member of my family. *Do not be afraid*, my father later pointed out. How strange that God says that and *keeps* saying it. Through the prophet Isaiah: Fear not. The archangel Gabriel to young Mary: Fear not. To the shepherds at Christmas: Fear not. Jesus in the Gospel of Luke: *Fear not, little flock; for it is your Father's good pleasure to give you the kingdom.* Perhaps *fear not* was not a peak-performance tip or a "nice-to-have." Maybe it was direct order.

✦

I suppose context calls for a confession of faith. Here are some verses from Romans 8:

> For we know that the whole creation groans and labors with birth pangs together until now. Not only that, but we also who have the first fruits of the Spirit, even we ourselves groan within ourselves, eagerly waiting for the adoption, the redemption of our body. For we were saved in this hope, but hope that is seen is not hope; for why does one still hope for what he sees? But if we hope for what we do not see, we eagerly wait for it with perseverance.
>
> Likewise the Spirit also helps in our weaknesses. For we do not know what we should pray for as we ought, but the Spirit Himself makes intercession for us with groanings which cannot be uttered. Now He who searches the hearts knows what the mind of the Spirit is, because He makes intercession for the saints according to the will of God.
>
> And we know that all things work together for good to those who love God, to those who are called according to His purpose.

MORE THAN CONQUERORS

For whom He foreknew, He also predestined to be conformed to the image of His Son, that He might be the firstborn among many brethren. Moreover whom He predestined, these He also called; whom He called, these He also justified; and whom He justified, these He also glorified.

What then shall we say to these things? If God is for us, who can be against us? He who did not spare His own Son, but delivered Him up for us all, how shall He not with Him also freely give us all things? Who shall bring a charge against God's elect? It is God who justifies. Who is he who condemns? It is Christ who died, and furthermore is also risen, who is even at the right hand of God, who also makes intercession for us. Who shall separate us from the love of Christ? Shall tribulation, or distress, or persecution, or famine, or nakedness, or peril, or sword? As it is written:

> For Your sake we are killed all day long;
> We are accounted as sheep for the slaughter.

Yet in all these things we are more than conquerors through Him who loved us. For I am persuaded that neither death nor life, nor angels nor principalities nor powers, nor things present nor things to come, nor height nor depth, nor any other created thing, shall be able to separate us from the love of God which is in Christ Jesus our Lord.

I prefer this last paragraph because it is easier, because it is more of a challenge. This hope in an irreducible unity of experience is not justified by any observable phenomena.

Yet it persists. Christianity also alleges that the energy that produced the world knows us. Wants us. Pursues us. Why? It likes us. (*And God looked at what was created and saw that it was good.*)

Unlike us, however, God seems rather ambivalent about creature comforts. He promises we shall lack for nothing but also recommends we give everything he's given us away. Because every thing has a price. Truly every thing seen, made, or said— socks, babies, nuclear warheads—costs something. And someone will pay. May not be you. ("Life is unfair.") Christianity maintains that God is not blind to these prices and understands the importance of showing up to pay them.

They call it incarnation: Jesus showed up. In person. (No messages in bottles.)

But Christianity's most offensive tenet by far has nothing to do with the virgin birth or the resurrection of the dead, but the first half of John 3:16: *For God so loved the world.* There will never be proof of that, though some see it in trees.

How can we know this God exists? We cannot. Only that sometimes, some days, some of us sense an absence, which feels very much like presence. It stings the eyes, we blink, and see lights and heroes all around us.

✦

In New York you try to make enough money to fly to other places, get away for a while, but airports don't function the way they used to. Instead of glamorous potential, airports now remind you more of your limitations, and so you seek solace in plastic-wrapped factory-made banana-walnut muffins and coffees too hot to drink before your plane boards. This works for a while, because too-hot coffee prods you to wait, sit, submit to this state of limbo. Wait for the world to catch up with your desires. Try not to stare at your phone and distract yourself from mortality. Put your own mask on before assisting others.

When blogs became popular I worried because no one else seemed as worried as I was. I was not worried about what self-publishing or everyone having their own websites would do to the quality of our discourse or democracy or anything like that. I worried there wasn't enough attention to go around, and that if everyone sought attention, there wouldn't be enough people paying attention, and for the system to work, a lot of people had to see themselves as attention-payers, not attention-getters.

Then suddenly it all seemed beside the point.

People still asked what my family imagined it was doing as missionaries. I still spoke of prostitutes, and how on our first Sunday in Holland, my mother drove our too-large Mitsubishi through the tight corners of the red-light district with Amy and me in the backseat. How she explained what these ladies sitting in the window wearing only underwear were doing, and how that was all she said on the subject. Maybe the job didn't look too appealing, so she didn't see a reason to caution against it. But the truth is that at bottom my mother hoped that if we were simply open to all people, the world would return the favor and free up some space where we could thrive. If we were nonjudgmental, others would be nonjudgmental, and loneliness would end for everybody.

Meanwhile my idea of what's sacred grows lumpen. Walking from the Canal Street subway station to my apartment late at night feels holy. The streets are littered with discarded paper napkins that hours before cradled coffees and pretzels. An aproned Chinese busboy squats on a stoop, hand cupped over mouth and cell phone, eyes on Hester Street and mind on a friend in Guangzhou. Drunk girls totter like baby deer in high heels, and they fling out their arms to hail a cab that will take them uptown, while down the block a man fingers for returned coins in one of the city's last graffitied phone booths. Stacked three feet high at the curb are black plastic bags full of evidence that earlier in the day hordes were fed food that perfect strangers cooked for them, and that they purchased designer handbags they knew to be fake, and also postcards and key chains and shot glasses that they will wrap in tissue paper and take home as reminders that their lives could have turned out differently, if only they had made different choices, if they had loved different people, if they had chosen a different city.

I know enough to know that tourists were scammed and

the seamstresses who sewed these purses were cheated and that dozens if not hundreds of children descended from sugar highs to throw tantrums and start bargaining with sweaty, tired parents: give me this Hello Kitty pencil case and I'll give you my satisfied silence. Because we never stop trying to strike that bargain, with everyone we meet our entire lives: let me have what I want and I'll tell you that everything is going to be okay, or that I love you, and really, there's no difference.

The black plastic bags will be gone come morning because green-uniformed men jump off the backs of trucks and grab the bags with gloved hands and toss them into the truck's belly, which is in motion and already advancing toward the next pile. And we'll do it all again tomorrow, gladly. We'll get lines around our mouths from the smiling. I tell myself that if God does not exist we would need to invent him, a proud parent to whom we could say *look, look, look* at all these things we can make. See how we persevere.

A letter Orville sent our family in 1984: Holland sounded very interesting, and he and Marian looked forward to their visit. In fact, he added, they would enjoy Holland thrice. First in anticipation of traveling there, then in being there, finally in recalling the hours spent there. In this blunt fact of neurological wiring he perceived a great gift from God. Time travel? We did it all the time.

And for him the promise of heaven was not clouds and perfect serenity but that past and future become unified.

When we were very young, we wriggled out of excess hugs. My mother clasped our hands during lulls in long sermons for three quick squeezes—*I. Love. You*. We squeezed back twice—*How. Much*. Then from Mom one loooong strong squeeze, hard enough to hurt. *Thissss Much*. She kissed us loudly on the ear without warning. *Mwahs* to rattle our eardrums. *Ow*, we'd protest, and turn around scowling, indignant, hand cupped protectively over the ear but always too late.

"Tough yuck," she'd say. "That's what you get for being so

blasted cute." SWAK—Sealed with a Kiss. An acronym for children who lick envelopes and dream of secret gardens and time travel.

Even then we realized, in the way children know things they can't possibly have learned yet, that very few people we met throughout our lives would feel compelled to kiss our heads. Not our lips and not our cheeks, but the tops of our heads, ears, temples, foreheads, noses, and sides of our heads, so that our hair stuck to their mouth, which was unpleasant but they wouldn't mind because they loved us so. Compared to this love, the outside world was downright hostile.

Loving someone and preparing them for the world are usually the same thing, in practical terms. But not always.

On a Sunday I visit my parents, we see this passage printed in the bulletin: "We believe that God created the family as the primary community of love and care. We pray that the light shining in our families might be used to brighten the world so that many will come to know and enjoy the Heavenly Father. Amen." Is it difficult for them to read that? I wonder. *It's interesting*, I say, on the ride home, because the Gospel seems fairly anti-nuclear-family to me. Considering all the bachelors that Jesus had hanging around him, all the single ladies, one a probable prostitute, and the verse in Luke to the effect of *If anyone comes to me and does not hate father or mother, wife and kids, etc. they cannot be my disciple.* And Matthew 10:35–36: *I have come to set a man against his father, and a daughter against her mother, and a daughter-in-law against her mother-in-law; and a man's foes will be those of his own household.*

Huh, my mother says. She never thought of it that way, and it's so interesting to hear how I think about these things, so different.

This is her way of telling me it's okay, I'm okay, and this loneliness will end for everybody. She will continue to believe that. Everyone soaks in a bathtub whose stopper doesn't quite fit, and the porcelain sides cool the water too quickly, and hot water turns lukewarm within minutes. We all emerge from the tub and stand dripping wet, clutching ugly towels, at some point in our lives.

So if we really wanted to show mercy, we'd create spaces wherein people felt free not to be impressive. Nothing is more terrifying than being loved and admired for your accomplishments, because one day those accomplishments will end, and with it, that love that didn't even deserve the name.

True mercy is not a matter of saying *We're not going to throw rocks at you because you committed adultery*, or *We're not going to lock you up for selling heroin*, but helping a body understand:

This is not a contest. There is no contest.

Or:

The contest is over. You won. Maybe you lost. It's hard to tell. But it's all the same to me.

And a person who has experienced mercy, and recognized it for what it was—mercy, not luck or the fruits of their charm—can never be the same. Because the merciful don't track results. They are skeptical of data. They listen gently and hold doors open. Their effect on us is like the sound of music. They provide that lungs-full-of-air feeling a favorite song gives.

Here's the essence of the parable of the prodigal son: One son is dutiful. His brother, on the other hand, asks for his share of the inheritance while their father is still alive. He gets it, then skips town and blows it all on wanton pleasures. Eventually he winds up in a pigsty. Time to head home, he decides. His father recognizes him when he's still just a dot on the horizon and runs to him, throws his arms around his neck, and kisses him. He declares they'll celebrate, everybody, the whole household, a great big party. The dutiful son learns of his brother's return when he hears music from the party already in progress, and he confronts his father. *What the hell*, he essentially says. He spits on you and ignores you for years and you throw him a party? Where was *his* party, the good son wants to know.

The father replies that the celebration would go on because the son he thought was lost was found. And this story is initially unsettling because it tells us God is not fair, not in any way that human minds track. But they celebrated because restoration to family was the happy in every happy ending. The kingdom is a courtyard in which those who are maimed in body and mind have priority over those who walk straight.

If we could all be merciful, we would smile at melancholy strangers and inform them they had beautiful hair. We would ban most advertising. We would seek out the embarrassed among us and offer them relief. We'd snatch their embarrassment and cradle it, smother it in our larger, louder, more demonstrative embarrassment. We would hold our more trivial opinions in palms facing upward with fingers stretched parallel to the ground, which is to say, so loosely that when a stiff breeze blew them into the street we wouldn't rush out to collect them but instead watch them tumble away.

The idea that spirits go a-wandering anticipates our fundamental subconscious desire to connect. It knows that mute cravings are strong enough to grow legs and walk. That when we are incapable of making ourselves known, either because we can't leave the bed or because we've lost our tongues, some portion of us takes care of our business, and our business is tugging on shirtsleeves and saying *Hey, you, don't forget about me. Don't forget about me, because I keep you in my heart. Because my home is in our heart.* We twist in bedsheets, wrestling with solutions, and this fraction goes a-wandering and whispering, *Hey, hey, hey, I am here. I am always right here.*

I'm thankful for:

1. The Lord God + His Son
2. Many happy years of life
3. My parents + brother + sister
4. my husband Orville
5. my 4 children + grand children (and their husbands)
6. Mill Ridge + all who work + live here.
7. For food, shelter + clothing
8. Relatives + friends.
9. Warmth in winter & cooling in summer

ACKNOWLEDGMENTS

For a fuller picture of the early days of Trans World Radio, I relied on *Towers to Eternity* and *Let the Earth Hear* by Paul E. Freed. Quotations from Sophie Scholl's letters were taken from *At the Heart of the White Rose: Letters and Diaries of Hans and Sophie Scholl*, edited by Inge Jens, translated from the German by J. Maxwell Brownjohn. The TWR resignation letters were edited for sentence flow but are otherwise true to the originals. Further insight into TWR was kindly given by Bill Mial, Laurie Lind, Skip and Joan Britton, Stephen Freed, Dick Olsen, Mark Lowell, and Lois Miller. Toward the end there's a line lifted from Pierre Talec's *Jesus and the Hunger for Things Unknown* (New York: Seabury Press, 1982).

Permission to quote Jacques Ellul at length was graciously given by Jerome Ellul. Snippets of *Unshackled* scripts were lifted from *Unshackled: Stories of Transformed Lives Adapted from "Unshackled" Radio Broadcasts*, scripts by Eugenia Price and book revision by Faith Coxe Bailey (The Moody Bible Institute of Chicago, 1953). "It's not that the unghosted aren't good people" (p. 186) is paraphrased from Dorothy L. Sayers.

Thanks to Jay Barksdale of the New York Public Library for the use of the Allen Room, and to the MacDowell Colony for five weeks in the woods. Much is owed Melissa Flashman, David Rieff, Karen Palmer, Alec Hanley Bemis, and Mary Mann, warm and wonderful people all. I am grateful that my parents responded graciously to intrusive questions. This book wasn't their idea, and it wasn't their wish, but they bore it well. Thanks also to Paul Elie for shaking his head until I dug deeper, and to Sean McDonald and Emily Bell for their good humor and high standards.